TOWARDS RATIONAL BELIEF

ZIAUDDIN AHMED

BOOKSIDE Press

BookSide Press
877-741-8091
www.booksidepress.com
orders@booksidepress.com

CONTENTS

PREFACE

The whole idea of mental exercises is to start a process of self-analysis and examine deeply imbedded ideas and beliefs in a conscious and rational manner. The writer has been motivated to dig out the dark recesses of entrenched feelings and rudimentary innate knowledge, to try to rationalize them and put them on the table, and share with people who usually look at things from an angle of enquiry and a questioning perspective.

It is rather difficult to doff the garb one has been used to for so long. Old habits die hard, but for progress and development to proceed ideas should evolve to match the change accompanying the passage of time. Evolution of thought leads to progress, and a balanced evolution is necessary for a durable effect. Balanced evolution is brought about by incorporating experiences and time tested ideas of the past into the practice of the present. This may eventually bear fruit in the future. A new age perspective is needed for the examination of even the axioms of the past. There is no need to tamper with them as they are for all time. Yet their dimensions can be grasped differently and they can be understood in the context of the present situation, giving a new view to the existing scenario and a new glow to the future.

It is hoped that these Essays will be read with an open mind and be given calm and diligent thought before discard and rejection. Since each essay was written independently there may be repetition or duplication of some ideas, yet each has a topic of its own. The overall emphasis is on the universal mode of evolution in all aspects of life. This is the central and underlying idea of the essays. The target audience is all those who have started thinking about religion and religiosity and specially Islam since 9/11. Those young people who see themselves in the midst of ensuing rivalries of faith and cultures at different levels of society, who may have had to grapple with some sort of a cultural shock, especially when they move to a foreign land. Having to face entirely new situations they begin to question their deep seated beliefs and fears. The effect on each individual is different, some become reactionaries and fundamentalists, some lose all interest in religious thought and some take a non-caring attitude towards spirituality, while some want to consciously rationalize the teachings of it. The only way to handle such a situation is to re-examine one's ideas in a rational manner in the light of the present conditions. It is felt that evolution is an inherent necessity of Nature Itself. The essays try to surmise this conclusion by studying various subjects and phenomena around, so the study of it and the resulting effect on some phenomena is looked at in the essays. Readers looking for a different approach to Islam, and religion in general, will perhaps find the essays interesting and cajoling. As learning is a two way process it is hoped that an interaction can be established between various groups of ideas and philosophies of religion. The essays delve on many different subjects besides religion, but the basic idea is to look for evolution and development of ideas from a different angle.

Gone are the times when one could live in isolated compartments. Globalization has made it imperative to examine and understand others' point of view in an atmosphere of accommodation and tolerance. Each one of us has to first see our own ideas in the present light, and then adjust them to match the change.

The title ' **Towards Rational Belief** ', reflects the proposition of how

Rational Belief can be developed by one's knowledge of facts that one gathers during his life time, and how Faith evolves into Rational Belief. There is a basic difference between **Faith** and **Belief. Faith** is the idea one is associated with from childhood. Ideas that one has been taught by the traditions and practices and those that have been inculcated by one's parents, elders and one's surroundings. Now, as one grows older one learns and explores new facts in life. One starts to examine His/Her Faith on the scale of one's experience and knowledge. One questions, re-examines, and judges it on an independent scale, and rejects those ideas that do not conform to his/her standard of judgement and knowledge and replaces them with those that seem to be in line with logic and scientific truths. This then becomes one's **Belief.** One's **Belief** is deeply ingrained in one's personality and becomes His/Her standard of life. It is very difficult to change one's **Beliefs'. Faith,** however, may be changed and evolves into **Belief** after rational thinking. This is what the essays are trying to project.

Ziauddin Ahmed
Canada
2024.
tidylink@Yahoo.com

Chapter One
EVOLUTION—THE INEVITABLE PHENOMENON

*E*volution is a natural phenomenon of modification which can neither be avoided nor denied. There is, however, a difference between change and evolution. While change occurs with the passage of time on any scale, evolution occurs with the passage of generations themselves. Change, in some cases, can be avoided but evolution cannot. Change may be temporary but evolution is enduring. Change can be an instantaneous process whereas evolution proceeds gradually. Change can be a reversible phenomena but evolution is not.

Cancer is usually an uncontrolled cellular growth. Healthy metabolism on the other hand, is a controlled division and multiplication of cells into the next generation—taking into consideration and being subservient to the existence of the body they reside in. It is no less than a marvel of evolution that healthy cell division preserves this prerequisite of existence. For, if cell division became uncontrolled and was not to follow the principle of live and let live, both the cells and the host body would eventually be annihilated, as is seen in the case of cancer. Looking at it through another example—a cancerous process is like an uncontrolled atomic reaction, much like a bomb, which is unbridled release of energy— causing the destruction of both itself and the surroundings. Healthy metabolic evolution, on the same scale, would then be comparable to a balanced and controlled nuclear reaction, as seen in the process of the generation of electric power.

Having got the gist of the idea, let's see some evolutionary processes and how they affect our lives. Keeping within the broad perimeters of the topic only some religious and scientific examples are being quoted, although evolution can be seen to occur in different forms in almost all fields of knowledge. Entire human development is the result of this constant process, and it is observable in every facet of life, be it *thought, word* or *deed.* The very evolution of this triad of life i.e. thought, word and deed constitutes the development of the individual and subsequently the evolution of the entire human race.

Man has been transformed through the ages from being a cave dweller to a resident of skyscrapers. This has taken place over generations of evolution. The entire Universe is in a constant flux and is gradually evolving. What started with the 'big bang' – an instantaneous change—has evolved over the millennia and may eventually be proceeding towards the 'big crunch'.

The main conflict between religious thought and scientific study is the concept and propagation of *finality*. Religious preaching is based on the 'word of God', which is believed to be the 'First and the Last'. Which cannot be questioned, and of which there is no tangible proof either. Science on the other hand demands that every theory or hypothesis be backed by logical, mathematical or experimental proof. However, seen closely, both the religious and scientific ideas have themselves transformed or modified over the years in an evolutionary manner. Scientific evolution by its very nature, as just explained, is clearly visible and documented, hence more rationally and readily understood and accepted. The evolution of religious thought, on the other hand, is subtle and inherently more subjective to the mental psyche of the era. Both religious and scientific fields of knowledge are none the less, derivatives of, and influenced by each other. Whether they do so consciously and with a full understanding of the other's position and contention, or unconsciously, as a subjective reaction to it, is however, debatable. To elaborate this let us take an example from history.

The early church contented that man is the centre of creation and hence must also be the centre of the universe, around whom all other creation should in theory be revolving. So in the 'Ptolemaic system' the earth got placed in the centre and the sun and all other planets were thought to revolve around it. This was disproved by Galileo's experimental confirmation of the 'Copernican theory' of the Solar system. Human mind had to eventually accept the scientifically proven fact of a stationary sun with planets revolving around it, rather than the reverse, which was the established belief. The point to note here is, not that religion or its belief was wrong at the time of the inception of the basic idea, but that all of human awareness and knowledge gradually evolved and took account of the fact that, as more scientific data became available to man, the existing belief could not accommodate it and the old theory could not fully explain it and thus had to be revised. Something had to be done to understand and explain this new data. So a more profound theory was born which was supported by logic and reason and which could withstand and verify these new facts more rationally. Copernican theory was thus far more acceptable to the age of reason, and with Galileo's verification of it, had to be adapted sooner or later—though not without pain and suffering, both for the scientist and also for the proponents of Status quo. A higher and more evolved concept is one that is able to adequately explain the previously available facts along with the new data, either more comprehensively, or in a new light altogether. This acceptance itself establishes the evolution of all knowledge based systems, be they scientific, religious or any other. This is what that leads *towards rationality in belief*.

Let us now see how scientific theories themselves tend to evolve with the advancement of knowledge. An epochal event in the scientific field was Newton's Laws of motion and gravity. They gave adequate explanations of the phenomena of nature till the emergence of Einstein's theory of relativity, which changed the very idea of time and space and gravity altogether. The theory of relativity is but a more evolved concept that explains and confirms the laws of motion, yet at the same time comprehensively explains new facts about the behaviour of light, and the nature of space and time and the influence of gravity.

Let's take another example of evolution, this time from religious thought. It is said in the Genesis that – 'God created the heavens and the earth in 'six days' and on the 'seventh day' He rested'. The Qu'ran mentions the same concept of creation, but instead of days it mentions 'spans' of time. To quote verbatim it says.

It is God who created the heavens and the earth
And all that lies between them,
In six spans, then assumed all authority.
You have no protector other than Him,
Nor any intercessor.
Will you not be warned even then?

(Al Qur'an 32:4)

The concept of 'spans' of time seems more evolved and rational than 'days'. This is so because the mention of days restricts the thought to the common conception of a day, which is 24 hours. Spans, on the other hand brings to mind a period of time, not limited to 24 hours—as some phenomena must surely have taken a relatively longer period than others to accomplish and sustain. The narration of the Qur'an seems more profound and rational, and shows an evolution of the intellect itself. Also, ' assumed all power' is once again an indication of a more advanced concept than " And on the seventh day God rested"; for, surely the Deity is no earthling to be in need of rest due to depletion of energy after hard day's labour or the like. Further, the mention of 'and all that lies between them', gives credence to the fact that it is not only the material things that were created but others too, the significance of which was understood in a different context altogether—perhaps not conceivable by most people then. The idea of quoting the religious comparisons is not to show one inferior to the other, but only to point out the level of the development of rationality and evolution of the human thought process itself, and that the very understanding of concepts evolve with the passage of time.

One field of knowledge that deals with evolution of connected systems is the 'Holonistic theory', first proposed by Arthur Koestler in the 1950's and later adapted by Ken Wilber. According to the theory of Holostic hierarchy or holarchy, all things consist of *holons*. (A term coined by Arthur Koestler, and refers to an entity that is itself a *whole* and simultaneously a *part* of some other whole.)

These holons are complete entities and wholes in themselves. E.g. the alphabets of a language a,b,c,…These can however, evolve to the next higher holostic level and become parts of new holons; for example alphabets can be made into words, e.g. cat, bat, mat… which in turn become the building blocks for the next level, say sentences, e.g. ' a fat cat sat on the mat', and so on. Another example could be taken from science where it is seen that 'atoms' are holons as they are wholes in themselves. They are the building blocks for molecules, which once again are holons in themselves, but a stage higher than atoms. After further evolution and changes molecules can convert to amino-acids, which may then go on to build cells and so on and on. Now, each set of holons that evolves must contain the holons of the previous level. These new holons are different from the predecessors in as much as the previous ones have been integrated in them and have acquired something extra to establish a fresh identity of their own. They have in fact transcended the previous order and have acquired some more, new properties. The higher mode of holons however, cannot exist without containing the lower levels, but the lower ones can exist on their own even if the higher order of holons is destroyed. The higher the holons grow in the holonic hierarchy the more autonomous they become and their capability and value increases.

Let us see how this theory explains evolution – and, as we shall see in a minute it goes on to explore phenomena even beyond. Matter, the physical manifestation of the *Kosmos*—(this is different from the *Cosmos*, better explained in books on holonic theory. Briefly, Kosmos contains the cosmos (or the physiosphere), the bios (or biosphere), psyche or nous (the noosphere), and theos (the theosphere or divine domain). It is the cumulative manifestation of all matter, energy and even psychology of the Universe.),—It may be taken as the starting point for our understanding of the levels of holons. A higher level of development, or further evolution of *matter*, would be the holon of life or bio-physics. (In between these there may be some sub levels, but we are avoiding them for the sake of simplicity). The new holon, the holon of life has developed over the holon of matter, in as much as it incorporates the phenomena of self-replication and multiplication to the holons of matter. It would thus be a step higher up in holarchy, and would be the higher stage of the evolution of matter. The result would be the manifestation of *living organisms*, i.e. *plant and vegetation*. A further stage of advancement of plant life would be the incorporation of mobility in the holon to reach the next higher stage—*animal life*. A further evolution and rational development of some species gets to the next stage i.e. the holon of the *mind*. Here the holons of life have evolved to the stage where it has acquired the ability to think for itself. This is the stage of psychological interplay incorporated with the holons of the animal body. *Humans* are the manifestation of this stage of evolution in the holarchy. It seems that over the millennia some cognitive and creative phenomenon has evolved life from the unicellular amoeba to the multi-cellular animal. This holon of the animal by some process of 'natural nurture' and selective development has then been upgraded to the holon of mind. Now, as per the holonistic principle the holon of the mind cannot exist without incorporating and transcending the holon of the body, which means that for the mind to have come about it is essential to have gone through an evolutionary phase of the body. And only after the body went through the required steps of change and readjustment it got prepared to be incorporated in the holon of the mind. A process of sieving out the developed elements from among the multitude of animal species, and then their further evolution must have produced those ingredients that finally became the mind. In the process of sieving only the right size of the grain can pass through the opening, the bigger or coarse particles are held back by the size of the mesh. One starts with a large quantity of the material but by the time the process of sieving is complete only a very small portion of the original remains. Similarly in the process of holonistic hierarchy or holoarchy most of the mass of the previous holons that do not fit the qualifications of the next level, are either rejected and discarded or not considered for further evolution. Although humans may share over 95% of genes with chimpanzees yet are markedly different from them, and are surely more evolved and advanced along the scale of existence. Showing that only a tiny percentage of matter evolves to higher levels from the vast amount of the whole, and only that which has matured through the process of '*systematic evolution*'. Let us stop here for a minute and see how far we have come. It will be observed that for the holon of the mind to exist it needs to encompass the holons of the animal, which in turn must have advanced over the holons of plant and matter. And so, on and on it goes. Now, continuing further along the holonic hierarchy we reach the holon of the *Soul*; and finally, perhaps the *Universal Spirit*. The beauty of the theory of holarchy lies in the fact that it goes on to show how the development of higher level holons enhance the very essence of the holon itself. This means that where there is vertical growth there is also lateral advancement; meaning that with progress along the scale of ascent, comes the increase in capability to perform and finally to acquire the ability to self-improve. This is the consequence of the fact that with the growth in knowledge comes the increase of understanding and awareness and the overall expanse of 'self'. Each individual has a capacity to grow – physically, mentally and spiritually. A balanced diet and regular exercise promote physical well-being. Reading, learning and mental exercise promote mental development. A healthy attitude in life promotes a desire to self-improve. If this is done in a balanced evolutionary manner durable progress is achievable. To develop this healthy attitude life requires a balance in both the physical and the meta-physical domains of personality. This is only an attempt to familiarize the reader with the idea of holons. The whole theory of holarchy is a complete subject on its own and should be studied in detail to acquire an in-depth knowledge.

Let me repeat the above for emphasis as it is a central idea of the essay. Each individual has a capacity to grow – *physically, mentally* and *spiritually*. A balanced diet and regular exercise promote physical well-being. Reading, learning and mental exercise promote mental development. A healthy attitude in life promotes a desire to self-improve. If this is done in a balanced evolutionary manner, durable progress is achievable. To develop this healthy attitude life requires a harmony in both the physical and the meta-physical domains of personality. *As an evolving system progresses and reaches the stage of self-perpetuation, it becomes self-participating and self-directing as well. For, if it is not so, the result would be self-destructing and self-diminishing. Now, the tendency of self-destruction in an evolving system is a negative or detrimental trait, and does not serve the very logic of its existence.* Humans are also a part of this self-perpetuating system and are positioned at a very high level in the whole spectrum of evolution—whereby they have gained the capability of being conscious of the system itself. They may not fully appreciate or understand the purpose of the system of which they are a part, yet they are aware of it and know that such a structure exists. They probe and search for its meaning in every thing around them. As said elsewhere, they do so by the use of their most important and uniquely private tool – the mind. This mind however, like most things, is a double-edged sword. It generates both positive and negative thoughts. It is both creative and destructive. It has the power to both accept and reject. All this in turn, depends on the basis of the thought itself and ones approach to the subject. If the basis or origination of thought or conscious analysis is positivism and open mindedness, it will endow progress and bear constructive results. But if the idea takes birth in doubt and deceit it will promote negativity and resistance to progress. Let us take an example. The splitting of a heavy atom (fission), or joining of two small atoms (fusion), releases tremendous energy. This release of power can be utilised either constructively, e.g. to generate electricity; or destructively, e.g. to make a bomb—depending on the purpose in mind. Interestingly enough, however, the process for electrical power generation is based on the principle of a controlled and balanced nuclear reaction; whereas a bomb is uncontrolled release of energy. This points to the fact that perhaps progressive processes are usually harnessed, balanced and controlled activities – or 'evolutionary in their nature.' Uncontrolled reactions can be catastrophic.

All stable systems in Nature have one thing in common—they are all balanced and evolving. A controlled evolutionary change is perhaps more enduring and longer lasting than a violent revolutionary one. Observe both the macrocosm and the microcosm. The solar system maintains its stability because it is balanced and evolving. At the other end of the spectrum of the Cosmos, the classical atomic structure follows the same principle of balance and poise. The greater the dawn of awareness, the greater the wisdom and the attainment of balance and, the more the elevation of poise. Sages, Monks, Sadhus and perhaps Prophets are a set of people that demonstrate this. They seem to be that group of individuals who have harnessed the tumult of material desires and mental agitations and reached the balance of mind, body and soul in order to acquire a poise of serenity. They are evolved souls who have reached the next level in holonic hierarchy. They would surely be a holon level higher than common human beings. Their next step would then be the holon of Universal Spirit -- where all souls would perhaps integrate and acquire the oneness with *Nature* itself, perhaps, the final stage of the great Holarchy.

The birth of an idea itself may be instantaneous or revolutionary in nature, but its establishment as a durable concept has to be nurtured and groomed by a process of slow and gradual evolution. We thus infer that balance and evolution are not only the keys to a successful existence; they are also its basic principle. It is thus safe to conclude that evolution is the inherent *nature of Nature.* It is It's very principle of existence and sustenance, and that advancement in any field of knowledge is the result of it.

Chapter Two

ULTIMATE HUMAN REACH

The quest of humanity

It has always been human quest to achieve *immortality*. The shape and form this manifests itself in is debatable, but its essence and concept are in conjunction with the design of their nature. That this is so is supported by some common observations, e.g. 'self-preservation'. This is by far the most basic of human instincts and is an everyday occurrence. There is no sacrifice one would not give to continue to hold on to *life*. All human struggle and endeavour is directed towards the keeping and preservation of it. Apart from one's own life, the only other more precious thing is the life of an offspring. In some instances the child gets precedence over self, especially in the case of a mother—the very source of that life. A mother is so protective of the offspring that she is willing to sacrifice her own life for that of her child's. Does this not show that the flame of life is to be preserved, and kept alight at all cost?

To be kept constantly and continuously burning, the originally kindled flame (of life) would have to be passed on from generation to generation—from the past, through the present, and into the future. This is done by a natural cycle of transfer of the *'essence of survival'* from the parent to the child. And it is in the instinct of creatures to treat this gift or blessing of *Nature* with the utmost care. Every generation nurtures, grooms and evolves this essence of life and then passes it on to the next. It thus appears that one continues to live through ones off springs; and so the spinning wheel of existence keeps turning. Is this not some form of continuity leading to immortality?

If this be it, then how and why it is so?

Let us examine the weave of life and its pattern. Perhaps it may give some clues.

Removal of conflict

Humanity has transformed and evolved through the ages. It has developed through a selective cycle of refinement and progressed through the art of living, over successive generations. This is an evolutionary process of gradually sieving and separating progress from decay—a method of preserving those qualities which aid in survival and sustenance and the removal of the destructive ingredients. The survival process actually promotes the growth of purities but hinders impurities. The underlying adulterations are separated and eliminated. For, only that which is pure and unadulterated can be a homogeneous '*Whole*', and thus be capable of existence without conflict. Hence the first rung of the ladder of immortality is the incorporation of a process for the elimination of conflict in the system.

Self-perpetuating System

In the evolution of a *self-developing* system, of which human beings is one, each generation differs from the past, and must change according to inherited or acquired principles to deal with the existing circumstance. Since the circumstance itself is changing, a new overall more advanced form comes to take shape with every successive breeding. The experience and knowledge acquired by the previous group is passed on to the next one by some means of transfer—genetic perhaps—to give to it the essence of its own invaluable experience and knowledge, gained and acquired in its own life time. Now, whether genetics can explain this is debatable, for the science itself is in its infancy. This information becomes the raw material for the future generation to face the challenges of their own, and thereby learn to keep their head above water. One thing however, to be kept in mind is, that the cultivation and propagation of 'good' or 'right' (meaning the sustaining and progressive forces), is far more laborious and demanding than the flourishing of 'bad' or 'wrong' (meaning the destructive or annihilating processes). This is so because the tendency of 'bad' to multiply is much greater, and the process to do so is relatively easier than that for the inculcation of the 'good' or the 'pure'. The destructive process is somehow revolutionary in nature i.e. quick acting; whereas the constructive process is evolutionary and slower acting in nature. Also, it is human nature to seek ease, comfort and pleasure, and the wrong provides this more readily and quickly. Seen in another way, the ideal path to success is just one out of the many, and has to be sought and sorted out from the so many other roads and traps lying on the way. This sorting and selection is a laborious and tedious task which takes time, effort, energy and perseverance. Taking any other way, out of the so many available, may not be the best way to the goal, though easy to acquire, it may not reach the desired end as properly. Hence, the change towards good although slower and tedious, is however, longer lasting and more durable. One concludes from this logic that in the long run, 'good' has the quality to eventually prevail over 'evil'. This is the apparent end towards which all religious philosophies are geared. Whose eventual aim being to inculcate in humans the sense of *auto-correction,* so that they learn to overcome the ill effects of things and continue to survive and thrive. Is this not a way to immortality?

The genetic effect

Modern thought and scientific advancement have illumined some interesting facts. The genetic code is a complete program of information contained at the cellular level. These cells are the building blocks for all life form. The self-contained code covers the complete life cycle of a being. Now, all species interact, multiply and propagate by communicating through the language of their genetic code. The information contained in the genes of an individual is the derivative of the exchange and interaction of information of its parents' constituents. The information in the parents' genes intermingles and produces a new 'compounded gene' of the individual being developed. That the new person is a compound and not a mixture is evidenced by the fact that the new personality, while showing traits of its parents, is a completely different entity exhibiting its own separate identity and individuality—beautifully blended, yet unique. What? and how?, the shape of the life will be depends on a number of variables, some tangible, like the physical traits of the parent, and some intangibles such as their emotional, mental and psychic predispositions.

The interplay of other factors like time, circumstance, environment and background of the parents also seem to shape the genetic makeup of the offspring. The exact traits the individual will acquire may not be precisely determinable, yet the overall effect of a group's collective behaviour—its cultural pattern and the influence of society on it—can be transferred as a common pattern of the whole. An honest hardworking group is likely to pass on the good habits to its next generation. Similarly, the bad traits of another group of people will most likely be picked up by its progeny. The study of genes and their behaviour has been mainly done in the physical field i.e. how genetic mutations result in the manifestations of different organs and organisms in both plants and animals. Genetics and is repercussions on the psyche and spirituality are wide open fields for research and development. A complete vista of knowledge lies untapped at the moment, and it is felt that information from this angle may revolutionize human thinking altogether.

The conquest of 'good' over 'bad' is again a process of conscious struggle with evil. Seeing the evolutionary progress of human development one concludes that this is in the *nature* of the entire creation. As noted earlier, survival is the first and most basic instinct of every living thing, and the action that each creature takes to preserve itself depends upon its makeup and its position along the hierarchy on the table of ability, with humans being at the top. *This means that human beings have the greatest freedom to affect change in themselves, their environment, and perhaps also beyond.* Now, as just discussed, the genetic phenomena is a natural process that is presently being studied and decoded by man; and that the genetic cycle is being experimented with and manipulated in order to study and observe the various outcomes. If the changes being made by scientists are in the right direction it will have positive effect and progress will have been achieved; but if the change is negative or detrimental to the natural scheme of things, the result will be degradation and eventual destruction.

If human interference in the genetic process is in conformity with the natural design of the system it will promote and aid in the development of the species as a whole, and they too will progress as a result. However, if human probes in the process are opposed to its natural sequence and direction, distortions will be visible along the way. They will eventually be eliminated as a consequence of the built-in *inviolability* of the overall *natural design* and its inherent quality of *self-preservation*. This in the end is the whole beauty of it. It is, in essence, this very same property that *Nature* hands down to humans in the form of Self-preservation and struggle for survival. They, over other living beings, have the added advantage of possessing an intellect —an instrument of probe, conscious enquiry, analysis, self-correction and subsequent conscious evolution.

Let us now examine some examples of things with evil effects and how humans can avoid and prevent their harm.

A Plan of Operation

Sex is one of the greatest of human pleasures, and its outcome is the greatest of their achievements, which is, *'the propagation of self, through the creation of another.'* In the past the outcome of the sexual act was mostly beyond human control. The general rule was that sex usually resulted in child birth. To keep the lineage straight and direct descending, from a selected ancestry, it had to be closely watched and monitored. Marriage was the institution for preserving and promoting racial heritage in the desired direction. The institution of marriage was thus sanctified and this sanctity was zealously guarded. That sex was a natural urge and desire, although denied by some schools of thought, could not be done away with. Thus to deal with it early marriages were invoked and sex outside of wedlock was shunned and abhorred. So sex became a taboo. Religion played the greatest role in influencing human sexual behaviour by propagating a code of morality all its very own, and linking it to the dictates of a *Super-human Reality.* This all encompassing Influence or *Existence* seems to operate under a *'grand master plan'* of its own by which it propagates various species. This plan is universal and valid for all time. Presumably, it is so basic that each and everything, animate or inanimate follows it subconsciously or instinctively. However, the case of human beings seems to be different. They challenge it and are bent upon changing it according to their mental makeup and intellectual curiosity. They may be able to do so, but first they have to decode and understand it, and fathom its meaning and essence. The main problem arises when human intellect gets to be egocentric, and claims to know it all. It then tries to decode the essence of the plan and the nature of the *Reality* despite the limitations of human knowledge and the inadequacy of facts available at its disposal. Other means of information beyond rational thought may hold the key to knowledge in that direction. The domain of instinct and/ or subsurface enlightenment may prove useful; because as we see that at those levels communication with Nature goes along the path of least resistance, and the information flows smoothly and easily from the sender to the receiver and vice versa. Thus intuition, sixth sense and perhaps revelation are a direct link with the mysterious *cosmic consciousness,* which is the metaphysics and essence of existence. This is so because consciousness prompts logic and reasoning, which act as hindrances or filters in the flow of information. Whereas at instinctive or subconscious levels reasoning and logic are bypassed. The case of Sages, Sadhus, Sufis and perhaps Prophets is a point to consider in the realm of direct communication with Nature. These elevated individuals demonstrate enlightenment of some or all aspects of Nature's functions and the wisdom behind it, and thus show more poise and balance in their lives. Most of us on the other hand are in a state of agitation. We have yet to learn the subtle communiqué and messages of our own natures which may be hindered by material distractions of life.

A fresh attempt to fathom the Plan

Keeping the above preamble in mind let's make a renewed effort to fathom *Nature's* plan of determining, directing and raising the creation to the level of *self-regeneration* and thus *perpetuation* and *immortality.*

17

It would make no sense if all creation was to have been meaninglessly brought forth and be then allowed to perish after having achieved so much progress and uplift in its psyche and spirit. To make some sense of all this apparent confusion and chaos has been the subject of all human curiosity and endeavour in every age and society. This is another such attempt in light of the direction of contemporary information and present human thought. (Refer to the essay 'Nature of a Natural Deity')

True purpose of Religion

Religious thought as discussed elsewhere, has itself developed and changed with human progress. The fundamentalists who practice religion in its most rigid form tend to stunt the growth of mental curiosity and intellectual probe because they limit and restrain man at a lower level and position God at a higher and altogether different station of abode. The one becomes the Creator and Controller and the other the subjugated and helplessly controlled. Also, religious orthodoxy inbreeds stagnation and unconscious ritualistic repetition. The natural outcome of unquestioned and blind ritual practice is introversive and becomes an end in itself, rather than being expressive, exploratory and a means to an end i.e. to lead towards self uplift and personal growth—which would surely have been its primary aim. Further, religious fundamentalism has negation as its basis. For it promotes religion by saying – 'don't do this',—'this is not allowed', —'that is against the rules'; etc. etc. Whereas the main aim of religious education should perhaps be to guide to the basis and the underlying need of various religious thought processes and disciplines and how they bring about self-amelioration. They should be able to advise how the practice of the ritual can lead towards its main aim of moral uplift and character building, which is essential for struggle and survival of a humane human race, and the eventual end game of 'good' conquering 'evil'. They should be able to explain how the prayer and worship are a road to the health and emancipation of the faculties of *mind, body* and *soul*—the triad of human existence. That their essence lies not in performing of certain tenets, but in effect the releasing of the constructive juices of each one's personality and harmonizing the functions of the human triad. That one may gain fresher ideas and thoughts and grasp newer concepts. These would then open and liberate the intellect rather than confine it. Religious education should be a means of accepting natural evolution rather than fighting it. It should teach to welcome rather than reject realistic change. It should be educative and helpful in training humans to be able to harness their animal nature and direct it towards humanism and progress, and to eventually overcome the barbarism of within.

Channelizing human Nature

A little closer study of humanity through history shows that humans continue to have the same basic animal instincts they have always possessed —both good and bad e.g. the instinct of curiosity, competition, instinct of self-preservation, protection, destruction etc. Only those who have been able to understand and channelize these natural behaviours have stepped ahead and furthered the cause of the entire human race. It may be questioned whether humans have really progressed? They are still the most brutal and ruthless of creatures. They still have uncontrolled lust, and in reality have furthered their lustful pursuit, and so on and so forth. *While all this is perhaps true, it may be pointed out that the basic instincts of human beings, because of their animal origin, will remain and continue to follow them. It is at the level of intellect that they can develop and advance, and its control over instincts improved.* This comes about through the progressive and refining process of genetic inheritance coupled with the reforming aspect of knowledge and education. The advance or progress can thus be made at the level of *'thought'*. If the thought or intellect progresses it will lead to a conscious improvement of *'word'* and then eventually *'deed'*. For, otherwise unconscious and untamed action is nothing but raw animal behaviour. Now, when intellectual development takes place, higher concepts can be grasped and understood and eventually put to use, contributing in the forward push of the frontiers of human achievement.

What will all this lead to, and what if any is life's final goal?

The shaping of Destiny

From an optimistic point of view, the entire human progress is aimed in the direction of self-discovery and conscious self-enhancement. This can be better explained by starting at the beginning i.e. going back to the story of creation as told by religious accounts. If, as is said, that man is made in the image of God, then it is through a study of himself, he may infer the nature of the *Deity*, and also perhaps the reason for his own creation. It is this aim and the pursuit of it that keeps man alive and kicking. If there were no purpose to life it would not have come about, or been brought forth anyway. Also the core of the existentialist philosophy of the 'meaninglessness and insignificance' of human life, becomes meaningless itself as it does not stand up to the scrutiny of the purpose of its own statement. However infinitesimal and apparently insignificant in comparison, each and every creature—from the gnat to a giant—has a position of its own in reference to its context in the space- time continuum. If the truth of the scientific fact – that no two things can occupy the same position in time and space at a given moment – can be fathomed, then the importance and value of each and every created thing comes to be accepted. Now the contribution of every being adds up bit by bit and the net result of all actions become the target for the subsequent act. This in fact is the gist of the moment and is shaped in the very mould of space and time. Consider it another way. An act of one affects another being or thing, which in turn reacts in some way of its own. This action and reaction produce a situation. The overall result of all the different situations forms a condition in time. At any given moment this condition of time is known as *destiny*, which is the net result of the action of one and reaction of all the others. This is thus being called the *'gist of the moment'*. In the realm of inanimate Cosmos the laws of Science and their application is relatively less complicated and the 'Destiny' equation is simpler, and various outcomes may be estimated or calculated scientifically or mathematically. Now, Destiny in humans is a dynamic process. For, what the act of one person will be depends on the exercise of his or her free will at that moment. What will be the outcome of a certain act depends on the reaction of the affected being, who in turn has a free will of its own, according to which he or she will react. Since there are so many variables along the way, it is not certain what the gist of any one action will be. However, it is undeniable that the more profound the action the wider is its repercussions. Also, the more appropriate the act, i.e. the right thing done at the right time, the deeper is the effect and thus the reaction. Total knowledge and information is the key, which in the case of human action is far more difficult to compute. While it is humanly impossible to tame all the information of a given moment and manipulate it to affect destiny, it may be possible by some *Divine Entity*. And again, only by that Divinity which is 'imminently indispensable', and is the inherent necessity of all things and every thing. Being fully aware, conscious and knowledgeable of all happenings, all the time. (This idea is discussed in more detail in the essay , ' The nature of a Natural Deity').

Derivation of Inferences

As discussed earlier it is human nature to seek pleasure and ease, and if this pleasure can come easy so much the better. Non- marital sex provides the fulfillment of such a desire. Giving pleasure and at the same time ease of freedom from responsibility and restraint, which are a natural outcome of marriage—a family and its subsequent responsibilities. However, as we have discussed, progress and development do not come lightly, and that the species would not develop to their full potential without the time constrained incubation and maturing of the genetic cycle as a whole—generation after generation. The process of passing through the passage of history, with all its informative and educative impact, has been an integral part of human uplift and progress. All the happenings of the millennia past have played their due role in bringing humanity to the current threshold of existence.

It is in the interest of the *Deity* Itself that sex be declared a taboo, because as we have seen, indiscreet sexual pursuits are an adulteration and detrimental to the promotion of a genetically unadulterated breed. This is needed for the development and accumulation of *Purity* that is a prerequisite of *Unity*, which as mentioned earlier is imperative for getting to a homogeneous *Whole*. So perhaps the 'grand master-plan' itself promotes the human code of morality.

Now, even today we are as vulnerable to the fury of nature as we were in the infancy of civilization and all through the process of history. Yet, the great difference is that our understanding of these phenomena has improved and we have developed newer means to protect our survival. We have nonetheless, also learnt about new means of self-destruction. It remains to be seen how we will fare with the passage of time. Were we to annihilate all we have so laboriously achieved, it would annul the whole idea of the elaborate process that Nature takes us through. As noted earlier this would be an exercise in futility. The fact of the matter is that human beings are slowly gaining more awareness of themselves and their environment with the passage of time and expansion of knowledge. They are learning new techniques and developing new methods to accomplish old tasks more efficiently and with more precision, and as a consequence are moving upwards on the scale of awareness, both in the micro and macrocosms. The zenith of all their achievement would be to learn to replicate themselves, thereby achieving *perpetuation* and thus *Conscious Immortality*. So the only logical end would be a culmination of the experiment of self-discovery to the level of self-replication and a full appreciation of *Nature's* 'grand master plan'. Whether this is at all possible is another matter, for there are a number of pit falls along the way. However, if human effort towards immortality is achievable then the *Image* would have attained the secret of the *Source* and thus become capable of conscious participation in Natures scheme of evolution.

Reflect on what Ghalib says about the strength of desire and the attainment of it, in the beauty of the following verse:

Waa kar diayay hain shouq nay bund e naqaab e husan Ghair az nigaha abb koi hayal nahin raha.

Desire's intensity has set apart,
the drawn veils of beauty.
Except for the sight itself,
Now, there is no hindering entity.

(The desire is so strong that it has penetrated even the cover of the veil, and the true nature of the beauty has now become apparent. The vision is so near and clear, that except for the eye itself, there is nothing to hold back the view and perception.)

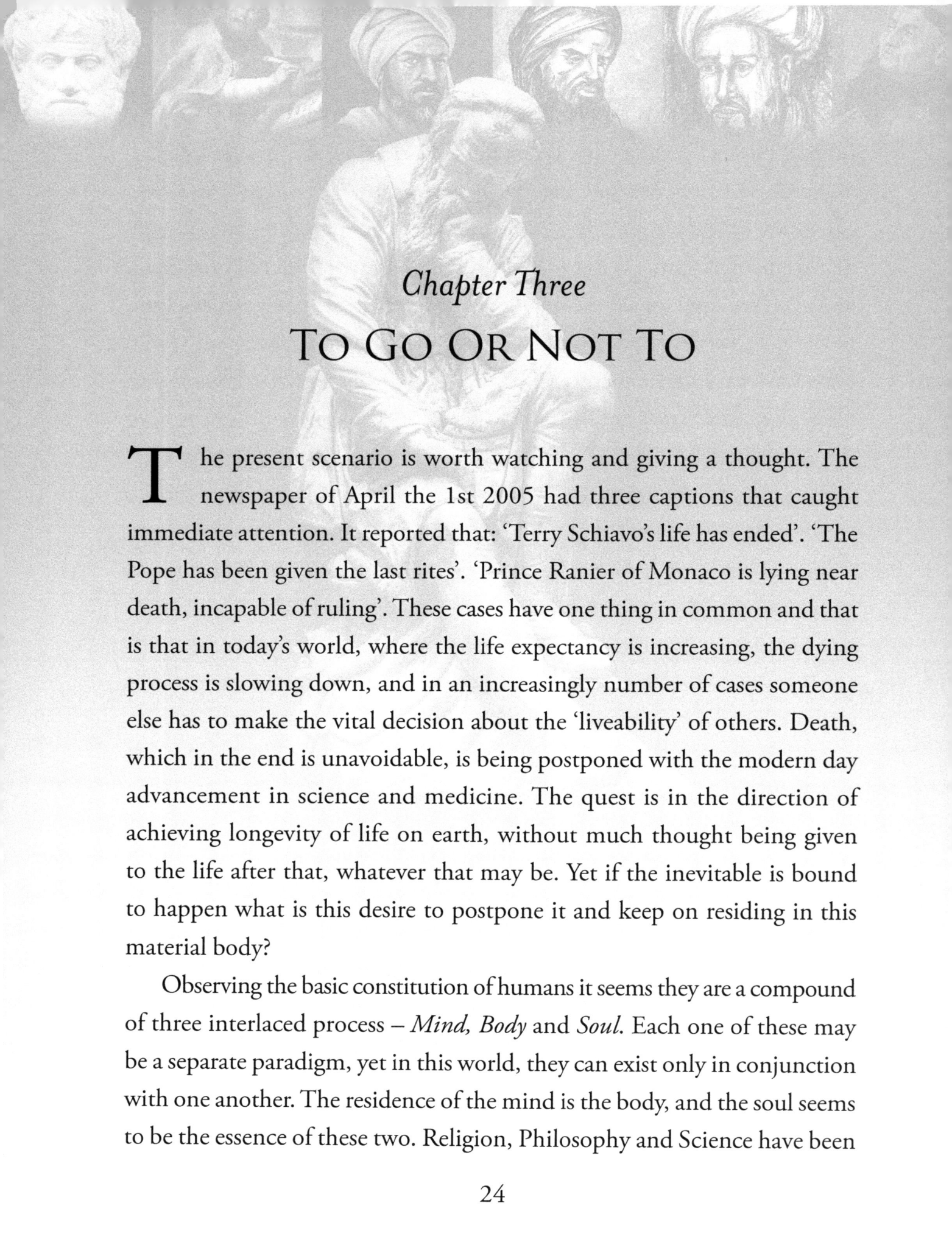

Chapter Three
TO GO OR NOT TO

The present scenario is worth watching and giving a thought. The newspaper of April the 1st 2005 had three captions that caught immediate attention. It reported that: 'Terry Schiavo's life has ended'. 'The Pope has been given the last rites'. 'Prince Ranier of Monaco is lying near death, incapable of ruling'. These cases have one thing in common and that is that in today's world, where the life expectancy is increasing, the dying process is slowing down, and in an increasingly number of cases someone else has to make the vital decision about the 'liveability' of others. Death, which in the end is unavoidable, is being postponed with the modern day advancement in science and medicine. The quest is in the direction of achieving longevity of life on earth, without much thought being given to the life after that, whatever that may be. Yet if the inevitable is bound to happen what is this desire to postpone it and keep on residing in this material body?

Observing the basic constitution of humans it seems they are a compound of three interlaced process – *Mind, Body* and *Soul*. Each one of these may be a separate paradigm, yet in this world, they can exist only in conjunction with one another. The residence of the mind is the body, and the soul seems to be the essence of these two. Religion, Philosophy and Science have been engaged in trying to understand the mysteries of the correlation of this triad. Whatever may be the outcome of that knowledge, this much is certain that each one of the three are needed for the survival of the human being on earth.

The birth of the body is the starting point of worldly existence. As it develops and grows, so does the mind. We seem to start from an unconscious state and begin to seek awareness, where for example, the moment a child is born it starts observing and exploring its surroundings, and this exploration increases with the increase of mobility and sensibility in its manner. Consciousness wakes the senses, and the mind gets into gear and takes control of the body. Action is enhanced and modified with the acquisition of experience and mental and physical prowess. The total experiences of the mind, body and soul contribute towards the evolution of the individual. One's life gets fulfilled and one achieves serenity if the acts s/he performs are in consonance and harmony with the Natural scheme of things. If the actions are in conflict with 'Nature' the balance and the natural rhythm of the individual are disturbed and dissatisfaction results in his being. This feeling or sense of dissatisfaction may be conscious or unconscious, depending upon the person's level of self- awareness and his/her own 'conscientious' deeds. Conscience itself may be suppressed or put to sleep but cannot be destroyed. It is bound to prick once in a while and remind one of the past deeds.

Do all knowledge, awareness and experiences gathered in a lifetime come to naught at death?

This does not seem plausible, for if it were so, life would be an existence without a meaning. The experiences gained through the process of living this life are a prerequisite to awareness and knowledge, and this must continue to survive in some form or the other even after the bodily life has ended. Through education, some kind of knowledge and/ or awareness is achieved, which once acquired, remains in the 'overall system', even after what has been learnt has been forgotten. Meaning that at death, i.e. at the time of transfer of life to some other form of existence, this 'knowledge' must also be transferred or transformed and carried forth into the new phase. The nature and form of this new phase may not be determinable for the process of death is irreversible and so the information gathered after it is irretrievable in a rational manner.

What then is this desire to continue to live this material life and prolong it?

Tracing the history of humans in this world it is seen that they have been busy gathering information and knowledge from the start of their existence on the planet. This instinct to explore and learn is endowed in their nature. Then again, it is their nature to utilize the knowledge gained, for the betterment of their existence. This is why they exploit the surroundings for their advantage. However, the more they learn from their actions the more there is to find and explore. This compounding effect of knowledge sets in them the need, desire and motivation to prolong the experience of achievement. It is simply this addiction of the desire to increase, material or immaterial things in life, that keeps pushing human potentialities forward and they wish to continue to go on living. Also since they do not have any idea of the state of existence in the next life, if at all there is one, they wish to prolong this one to the maximum.

Cycle and change is a basic natural function. This results in evolution. Evolution itself is a link in the chain of transformation and/ or development of new forms or phases of life. As most phenomena in nature are continuous in the long term, so perhaps it would also be with existence. Life on earth begins, as we have seen, as a child. It develops and progresses, accompanied with change and modification for a certain time, eventually transforming upon death, perhaps into some other form of existence. During this phase it fulfills certain prerequisites for the onset of the next stage. The physical development of the body gets coupled with the overall compounding of other factors like knowledge and skill, and brings about an enlightened 'awareness' of the presence in the 'Soul' itself. The moment one dies this evolved soul is liberated from the constraints of the physical body. It goes to the realm of the metaphysical, taking with it the gist of the knowledge it may have acquired during the process of this life. It takes away the capability of consciousness and awareness and the ability to act. *The physical situations and the ability to perform deeds are lost and left behind, because deeds are simply the manifestation of the metamorphosis of the metaphysical to the physical in the form of a living body.* At the metaphysical level the soul may acquire the capability of 'cosmic awareness'. The more the soul may have been cleansed and evolved by the passage through this world, the more power it has gained to tune into the message of the 'Kosmos'. The soul gets purified by good thoughts and actions but gets adulterated by bad ones. In either case it evolves or devolves with the passage of time and life on earth. The soul has the inherent quality of knowing the good from the bad, and it cringes and shrinks at every bad deed and flourishes and expands by every good act. It is interesting to note that the Qur'an narrates this in vivid terms for it says:

The soul and how it was integrated
And given the faculty
of knowing what is disruptive
and what is intrinsic to it.
He who nourishes it
Will surely be successful,
And he who confines it
Will surely come to grief.

(Al Qur'an 91: 7- 10)

Now this 'Entity', the soul, consists of a 'Self' and an 'Over-Self', and the essence of the life on earth is the search of the Over-Self by the Self. The Over-Self in turn tries to align the Self and harmonize it with Itself. The secret of the mechanism of communication is not readily fathomable or attainable by all, and only the more evolved beings from among the humans may have acquired the taste of it. In other words man keeps looking for a God and God is in eternal benevolence to reveal Himself to him provided the search is in consonance with the design of Nature. This life has to be lived with all its ramifications to be able to fathom its own meaning and the reason of it. The entire quest of man is in the direction of acquiring the secret of this mystery. It should, however, be kept in mind that there is no uniform standard of achievement and development of awareness in humans, and that each person has the capacity to grow and learn in an individual manner. The general rule is that each species develops according to its inherent potential. In humans this potential is somehow affected by their 'free will' and strength of 'character'. Both of which, as said earlier, develop with knowledge and experience in life. Humans are different from animals in as much as they have the 'capacity to bring about an increase in their own potential'. This is the outcome of their being evolved in 'mind'—which is a phenomenon for improvement over and above the 'animal' phase of life. Man is thus capable of further evolution mainly in the direction of his mental capacity and abilities. The physical or animal phase of development in the human species seems to have peaked out, and further advancement in that aspect of life is to fine-tune or increase the efficiency of the existing bodily functions. We will not be able to grow an extra pair of hand or feet, but may be able to supplement and improve their functioning with inventions of more implements, instruments and medication that aid their efficiency. This is what has resulted in the increase of the average age of humans. Now that man has been able to see the possibility of increase of life he wants to continue to live longer, yet somehow forgetting or not fathoming that this life may not be the 'be all and the end all', but a stepping stone to other modes of existence.

There seems no harm in the desire to prolong life as long as the increase is progressive and productive i.e. that humans can continue to contribute towards the benefit of humanity and not become a burden on it and hence on themselves. The case in point is the Terry Schiavo's affair. It is interesting to note that the affected individual had no capacity to influence the decisions being taken for her by others, thus making her a pawn in the game of chess being played around her. This kind of living does not seem to be the purpose of life. Humans were not created to survive on feeding tubes and catheters. Whatever Terry Schiavo acquired by way of life, came to a standstill the moment she went into a coma. From then on it was for others, her kin, the doctors and the society at large to keep her alive for their selfish purposes, or for their learning and experimenting on human life itself. To give it the shade of love and emotion and to show the world one's feeling for the incapacitated is all very well, yet is it not true that 'anything and everything anyone does, does so for oneself'? This seems a very selfish statement, but is axiomatic none the less. Hence the prolongation of life of such individuals is not for themselves but for the learning benefit of others, who may perhaps put the knowledge so acquired to use for posterity. How are we to know what Terry Schiavo's personal situation was? Did she want the vegetative state to continue forever? Was there ever a hope she could be rehabilitated to live a life on her own—for which purpose we are all here in the first place? Whatever may be the answer to these questions it is evident that it was others who would have to decide this first, for and on her behalf. Terry Schiavo had become a guinea pig for the professionals to experiment, manipulate and manoeuvre. Such a situation and state of existence does not seem to be the natural scheme of things for any individual; because in the 'natural scheme' each and every thing has a place, purpose and a role to play, and then move on. It may be argued that perhaps this vegetative state was Nature's purpose for that person, and that perhaps it was her destiny to become an example for others to observe and learn from, and for humanity to benefit from the knowledge thus acquired. This is all very well from a fatalist point of view, but Nature does not seem to be fatalist. Nature is living and dynamic. It is constructive and progressive. It promotes survival and progression. All this can only be done and achieved if each part or constituent in Its domain plays an active part and having done so moves on, and does not hinder or hang on and continue to be a dead-beat and occupy space—which would have become vacant for some other, new, progressive and contributing element.

Now, if this line of reasoning is accepted then it becomes evident that man's position, being part of a self-perpetuating system, is to understand his/ her own capability, and then surrender to the dictates of Nature voluntarily; meaning that each one of us who is capable of understanding one's capabilities should make it abundantly clear how we are to be handled in situations where we become incapable of handling our own selves. We owe it to our self-respect and to others' feelings, and emotional attachments. This will spare both the 'suffer' and the 'suffered' the unnecessary pain by prolonging the agony of life which has become unproductive and also a hindrance for others.

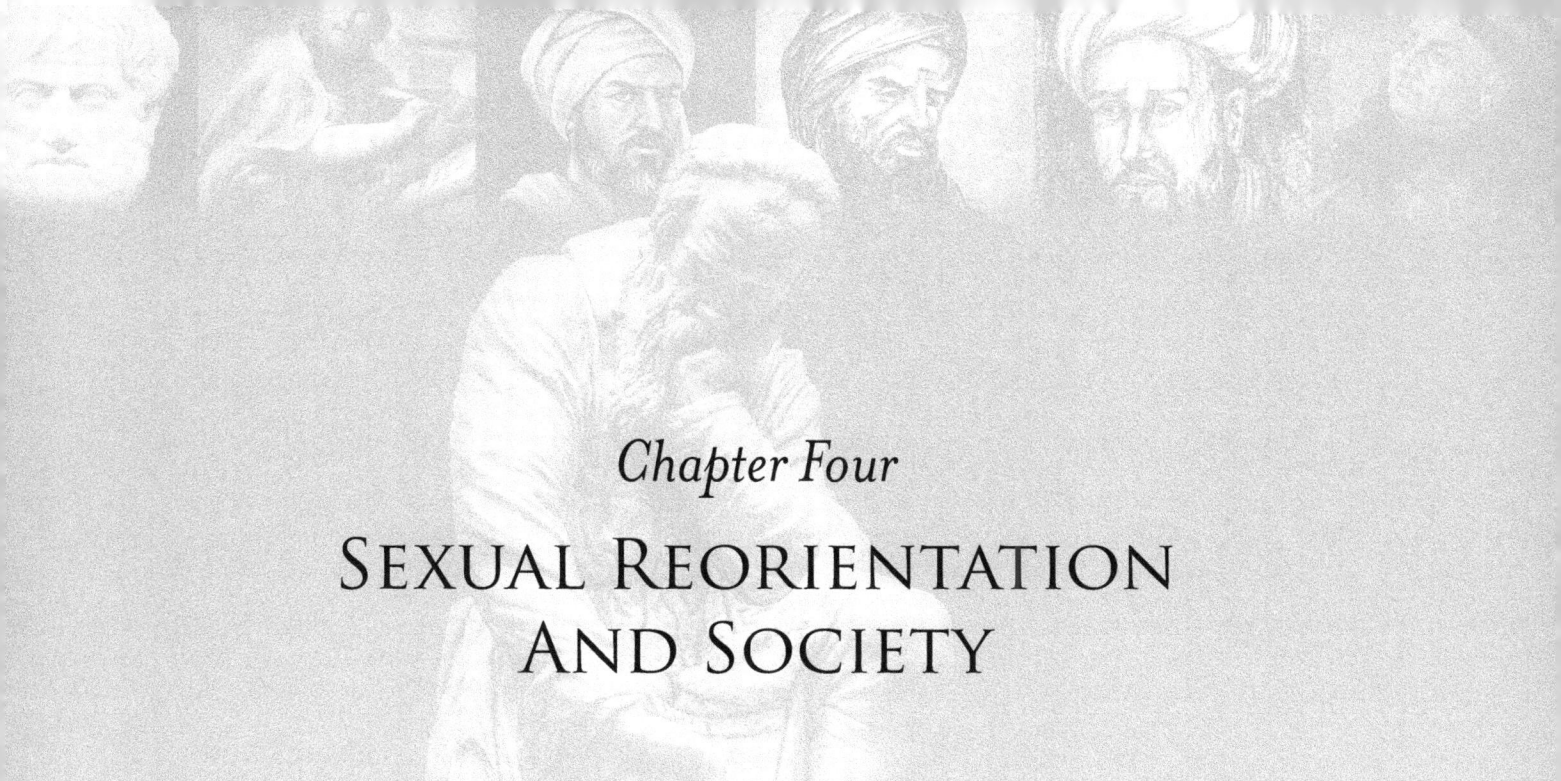

Chapter Four

SEXUAL REORIENTATION AND SOCIETY

To elaborate the impact of 'Sexual Re-Orientation on Society' and see the extent of change, I have endeavoured to peep into the future, but from a different angle – that is, to see it as phenomena of Natural Evolution.

In evolution the change of pattern occurs slowly and gradually. Evolution is a natural phenomenon that can neither be avoided nor denied. If everything has evolved over a period of time to the present level, there seems no reason why it will not continue to do so in the future also. Now, if this premise is accepted then 'to what' and 'how' humanity evolves, becomes a subject of educated guesstimate and speculation. One region to study would be the impact of 'human sexual evolution'.

Morality and religion aside, the primary outcome of human sexual exploits is a natural process of multiplication of the species. Were there no pleasure in sex, there would neither be the explicit desire nor the basic need for it. That there is extreme joy and satisfaction makes it a primary pursuit of human beings and also one of their coveted goals, of course only after the satisfaction of other basic needs of survival like nourishment, shelter etc.

The sexual act is a normal and natural phenomenon with the animals and comes instinctively to them. The performance of the act of mating is a rather personal affair and is usually performed in the private. This again is the way nature works. Hate has the desire to expose and spread openly; the tendency of love, however, is to seek cover, peace and privacy. This is due to its nature of self-fulfillment in an atmosphere of serenity and tranquility. What one is seeking here is beauty of nature and that beauty is enhanced if it seeps in quietly and in a peaceful and tranquil manner. Love becomes a vulgar and a repulsive act if performed on the public platform. A certain amount of secrecy enhances its charm and aesthetic value and a little imaginative admiration is an addition to its beauty. It is nature's design to keep the sexual organs under cover and when over exposed their ugliness becomes pronounced and they tend to lose their inherent integral beauty.

Humans are both physical and spiritual beings. They have to try and maintain a balance in these two sides of their nature. A one sided physical pleasure in the sexual act, without keeping in mind the spiritual aspect of it, disturbs this balance and leads to perversion and abusive tendencies. And perversion has no limits. This is seen in the modern trends of the material tilt of the human beings present lustful exploits, where the spiritual or the metaphysical aspect of their natures is being pushed in the background, and the physical satisfaction of sexual desires are coming to the fore front. To validate this contention one has just to see the present rise of pornographic activities, both in adult and child sex. Further, as sex is a natural desire and tendency of the life cycle of the animal, human practice and promotion of unnatural designs of Celibacy and Puritanism is not a durable design either. It is bound to break down sooner or later. This is becoming clearly visible in some religions, where the unwarranted abuses of the helpless and the week among them, is now coming out in the open. Another phenomenon that is being openly discussed these days is the abuse of the blood relations by their own siblings. This is perhaps a purely lustful or a psychologically distorted behaviour and needs be handled at that level. It may be true that in the olden days, both in history and mythology, marriages between brothers and sisters and even fathers and daughters have been recorded, specially in the ruling classes; but those were then justified to be the necessity to keep the lineage and the wealth and power secure in the family. The same practice seen in the animal kingdom may be condonable, but certainly not in humans. Incest in human relations cannot be justified at the stage of a developed and evolved species. The practice in the past too seems to have ended when it was seen that it did not well serve the purpose it was intended to.

Seeing the advancement of knowledge and its affect on human lives and their behaviour, it is worth noting that the sexual endeavours have also undergone a radical change. They are bound to get free of the past impediments of religious and social morality. From the primary source of reproduction, sex has now taken on a more explicit and glamorous secondary role of exploitation, entertainment and manipulation in many different ways. It is these secondary uses that have diversified and changed its position in priority, practise, and thus its very inherent nature. The approach to sex also differs between the genders, mainly due to their physiological make up and hence their natural demands and predispositions towards it. The male, by virtue of the fact that he does not play a major role in the incubation, birth, and the initial nurture of the offspring, does not attach as deep a value to the very act of sex or its repercussions. He usually gives more importance to the fetching, implementing and forgetting the relationship after its conclusion. The female on the other hand, being imbedded by nature for a longer duration of attachment to the outcome of the act, is naturally more intent upon longer term relationships and so she gets more sentimentally involved in the whole affair. Yet again, the gender distinction incorporates in each of them a difference in their roles of the enticer and the enticed, with the 'tender and more alluring' role usually shown by the female and the more aggressive and a 'matter of fact' attitude by the male.

What was primarily the function in the 'Foraging' and 'Agrarian' societies is seen to have radically changed in the 'Industrial' and then the 'Information' age. Heterosexuality was the naturally accepted mode of sex in the first two, as there was the inherent need to increase the 'pair of hands' needed to accomplish different tasks. This has changed in the Industrial age due to the promised advantage of machine over the sheer strength and numbers of manual labour. The Information society of the present times, with all its re-evaluation, in addition to experimentation and readjustment in every field, has changed even the male female equality role in society. This has led to the innovation and diversification of sexual pursuits. Coupled with the modern techniques of birth control and the means to the aversion of unwanted pregnancies, has changed the natural power over its consequences. This has thus altered the postponing of the inevitability of marriage itself. Call it a perversion or a need for change of taste, sex is now seen more of an exploit for pleasure than reproduction. Its need as a sole means of reproduction of the species too, is decreasing with the rapid developments in bio-physics, and with the explosion in the knowledge of genetics and pharmacology. Now, it is not pure speculation or scientific fiction to think that man may be able to replicate his species through artificial methods, besides the natural way of reproduction. Animals of various types have been successfully cloned and even human cloning has been reasonably well experimented. What is there to stop man from walking side by side with naturally born babies and those produced by scientifically cloned ones?

Seeing all this and with a possibility for much more, what is the need for dependence on Mother Nature for generating and keeping the sanctity or the purity of the descendents through the act of mating alone. Once the natural recipe has been decoded and understood it can also be manipulated at will to suit the desire and need of the individual. Made to order babies are now a conceivable possibility. The scenario becomes more and more interesting with the possibility of self- imposed and modified adjustments through scientific methods. One can now produce test tube babies on a made to order basis, by choosing the color of their eyes, the pigment of their skin and may such changes according to their wish and whims. Since the need for reproduction and propagation of the human race is now becoming manageable by man himself, there is apparently no need for the past naturally imposed bindings of relationship between a male and female. This is evidently seen in the progress of homosexuality and same-gender attachments. Time is very conducive to take up our destiny in our own hands and see how many combinations besides heterosexuality can be promoted. The accepted homosexuality, both gay, lesbianism, and transgender relationships are becoming an everyday affair. There remains little reason for debate of whether heterosexuality is a natural or acquired desire for sex, because as just seen, its primary need for human reproduction is well on the way of being satisfied by other means. So shouldn't the way of looking at sex itself be modified? It seems a natural progression in the evolution and readjustment of human thought and behaviour. This change of gender relationship is well established. The capability of 'marketable child production' is now a reality, and child production may not be restricted to male and female copulation. Now, is this not ample reason to justify the diversification of the sexual relationship and its methods? When the natural need of reproduction can be satisfied by other means, does it really matter who weds whom? The very institution of marriage has become questionable. Yet the natural affinity for relationships will somehow keep the concept alive in one form or another.

The need to hold on to the traditional nuclear family structure with all its ramifications is also changing and evolving according to evolution in the means of production and reproduction. The very concept of the old 'nuclear family' is under scrutiny and debate, leading to a new vista in relationship of the sexes. Now there is need to look at other various limitations and the resulting readjustment of the total human psyche, based more on the changed idea of a family and its meaning in society. The traditional family structure was a necessity of the earlier mentioned Foraging and Agrarian cultures, where the division of work was on certain distinct lines. With both men and women participating and contributing equally in the present day societies there is hardly need for the closed ended family unit of the past. Also as a result of the change of the nature of work itself, there is the inevitable necessity for the female gender to excel at the work place, and establish themselves as equals and perhaps even superior in some fields. This is a result of the female's liberation and entrenchment in every mode of life's functions. The complexion of the society is bound to readjust. What will be the impact of the rupture of the traditional family set-up is difficult to pin point, but that it will shake up the very foundations of society are none the less being felt even now. Imagine the full establishment of women equality and undoubted excellence in some fields that are at present primarily male dominated. This is bound to make the male look and rethink his position and standing on the world stage. His male chauvinistic attitude which had kept him in a superior position of strength is bound to be reshaped in some way. The females, by virtue of their cooler and perhaps more sublime temperament, show a longer enduring tendency to better withstand the changing challenges of the modern pressures of life.

The resulting change cannot be analysed in isolation because the very fabric of human society will be drastically affected. If however, the change is basic in nature, as it is bound to be, it will not easily be accepted by the entire species in one go, but only bit by bit and in digestible portions. This change can only be sustained through an evolutionary process and through overnight revolution. As we have seen that since evolution itself is inevitable, the present scene is in for a change, though it may not all be possible to predict. It may take just a generation or two to see the world as a very different place to live, one that may be on a completely different standard from today.

Chapter Five
OPTIMAL MARRIAGE

Marriage is a meeting of the mind, body and soul of two individuals, and any fruitful marriage occurs in the same order—mind, body and then soul. When two people wed it is really the start of a meeting for a lifetime. This meeting may either become a 'clash' or a 'blend'. If it is a clash the result is loss for both, but if a blending takes place then the outcome is the development of a healthy and a life-long partnership. A marriage becomes a clash when the two do not see eye to eye on most issues and one tries to impose a one-sided relationship on the other. An accommodative attitude of each partner leads to a blend of the triad of the family of man, woman and child.

The institution of marriage serves various purposes for the individual, depending on one's understanding and desires in life. In the natural scheme of things marriage would be a harmonious relationship between two people to flourish and develop as they grow and mature. For this to be fulfilled it requires that both parties agree to cooperate on the basis of equality.

In a successful marriage each partner has both to give as well as take. If the willingness to give is more than the desire to take, the result is a prospering of the relationship. For, in giving willingly the end result is usually beneficial to the one who gives, as in the long run the receiver is bound to reciprocate usually with more than expected. What one spouse gives does not get lost; it only goes into a 'joint account' of the family, so to say. The contributions made by either partner may not be of equal material value, but their worth should be measured by the intent and spirit of the effort in which they are made. If both spouses contribute to an 'account' it will grow. On the other hand if one takes too much, he/ she over draws and depletes the savings in the 'family's bank account'. If the spirit of cooperation is considered in this manner then each good act by a partner towards the other is in a way a positive investment for a mutual benefit. Remember that love has the tendency to grow and multiply, just like the savings; whereas, hate shrivels and shrinks, just like any wasteful expenditure. Love is inculcated by looking at the positive points in the spouse, whereas hate breeds by seeking and criticizing the shortcomings of the other. As for every thing else in life the maintenance of a balance is the key to success in a marriage.

If one spouse gives, the other is bound to realize one day that most of the contribution in the 'savings plan' has been done by the other, and he/ she would surely think of compensating for the lack of contribution in some form. The return may not necessarily be in the same coins, and can take various shapes. E.g. A husband's good reception by the wife, on return from a hard days work, may be repaid by a congenial and loving evening together. The cleaning of dishes after a meal by the husband may prompt the wife to make his favourite dish the next time. It is really such small things that become the building blocks for a strong, concrete and a loving home. As it is said, take care of the nickels and dimes and dollars shall take care of themselves.

In the building of a strong bond the most important thing is honesty. Any relationship built on the principles of honesty will withstand the toughest test of time, for each one of the partners will then not waste their fruitful energy in pretending or covering up their own mistakes, or resisting one another just to prove a point. Both will work together jointly for seeking a solution to the problem facing the family. The next building block of married life is trust. This is gained over a period of time, and if one remembers that the other is as much a part of the household as oneself and needs to be recognized and encouraged for whatever role he/ she plays in the home, the whole structure will be built on a solid foundation. This will lead to an appreciation of each other's worth and the strengthening of the family unit.

That this position of equality is not being given in some societies is surely against the spirit and essence of the message and by no means a correct practise or interpretation of it. The strength and importance of this equality between the male and the female is shown and highlighted in accordance with the nature and structure of the man and the woman. Each has both a separate and collective role to play in the making and the raising of a healthy family. The central idea of marriage is coordination and the division of duties and responsibilities, and thus the building of mutual respect between husband and wife. The capabilities of male and female may differ in the 'execution' of the various tasks. A woman's duties as a wife and a mother are in no way less important than the functions of a man as a husband and a father, a wage earner and protector of the family unit. That this fact has been misunderstood and misinterpreted over a long time in the history of marriage has led to the chauvinistic attitude in the male who kept the dominance of the society for so long. This is being challenged only recently by the other half of the human race. Although the traditional roles of the husband and wife may have seen a lot of change over the years, yet the basis of love and understanding remains the same i.e. honesty, trust and goodwill. In the changed conditions of today's society it is most important that both should be considered as two wheels of a bicycle, where the front leads the way, yet, if the rear is not to push, no distance would be covered. In the present times of great demands and stress, it is most important to confide in each other and never to stop consulting on matters of mutual interest. Democracy has been seen to be the best policy in most walks of life, so why not in marriage.

The institution of marriage has been sanctified by every religious order. Of the three monotheistic Abrahamic religions, Islam is the last to evolve out of the previous two; and in evolution it is imperative that the previous orders are incorporated and carried forward. A critical analysis of Islamic thought shows that this is in fact what has happened.

Marriage in Islam is a civil contract made between two consenting adults. Each party to the agreement has equal rights and obligations. The equality of the sexes has been quite explicitly dealt with in the Qur'an at various places but especially in Sura An Nisa, its fourth chapter.

(4-1) O MEN, FEAR your Lord
Who created you from a single cell,[1] (Arabic *nafs*)
And from it created its mate,
And from the two of them dispersed men and women (male and
female) in multitudes. So fear God in whose name you ask
of one another (the bond of) relationships. [2] (Arabic *arham*)
God surely keeps watch over you.

---

1 Note that the cell is a complete unit or an entity by itself—in itself a 'nafs'. Since both male and female have the same cellular origin, it gives absolute equality to women with men. This point is emphasised throughout the Qur'an. The mention of—and from it created 'its mate', (note the neuter gender)—points further to their similar origin, and once again their equality.

2 And further,—The arham or bond of relationships, and the symbiosis (harmonic association of different organisms) implied in the verse, make the equality of man and woman even more significant and completely beyond doubt and debate.

The orthodox and dogmatic tradition may choose to interpret things differently, but it does not mean that the basic natural axiom can be changed or demolished and/ or submitted to the dogmatist's interpretations alone. Their propagation of the message is primarily based on the concept of fear. This concept of fear is itself very frightening indeed. It leads one to think that God should always only be feared. This in turn makes Him a terrifying and repulsive Deity. But if we observe the time and context in which a certain thing is said, it may make more logical sense. Arabia was a male, chauvinistic, an uncouth and a ruthless society. The fear of reprimand was perhaps the best way to restrain it, and was the only effective language the people of the period understood. The traditions of culture and society were not subservient to the dictates of logic or reason. Even now, we sometimes have to use fear to keep humans in line. E.g. if there were no fear of punishment built into the Legal system many would flout the Law quite conveniently, and get away with murder, so to say. The two psychological tools of fear and reward, used effectively may be enough to reign in the unbridled creation, and this is seen to be done throughout religious preaching in human history. Even the basic law of 'cause and effect' had to be explained with the examples of punishment and reward e.g. if one does wrong the punishment is 'hell' and if one does good the reward is 'heaven'.

A natural outcome of marriage between a man and a woman is the propagation and increase of the human race, and they, consciously or unconsciously participate in the evolution of it through their off springs. However, in this regard each spouse has both duties and obligations. On the one hand the male is required to restrain his extramarital pursuits and devote time to the raising of the offspring, and, on the other hand the woman will have to take up the most important task of not only bearing them but also rearing them initially. This task of the woman has been downgraded and called menial only due to the chauvinism of the male. However, in the natural scheme of things this is perhaps the most important and valuable task assigned to humans. This initial period of devotion from the parents is the not generally correctly understood. The baby's period of unconscious development is the most pertinent for its life on earth. The knowledge and awareness the baby absorbs in its infancy is done at a plane of gaining information through subtle and unobservable means. It is nature's way of providing the child the much need knowledge for self-preservation. Most parents do not have adequate knowledge about this or are perhaps distracted by their own selfish pursuits and tend to remain unconcerned about it. The upbringing of a child requires sacrifice by both parents and a long-term commitment besides other pursuits of worldly pleasure. This duty of humans to his children and consequently to themselves is the basis of evolution of self and the society as a whole. This, when understood fully entails that the unnatural trends of modern material society have to be resisted and channelized i.e. the thinking has to be readjusted to making the family unit the centre of one's life. In so doing they are duty bound to think of the welfare of children, first and foremost. Remember that we live through our off springs and thus seek immortality. (This idea has been discussed in the essay, 'Ultimate Human Reach'.) The parents have to realign their individual desires to make the family unit the basis of future lives. That this in being sidetracked and distracted by the need of placing the self ahead of the natural design, which requires sacrifice and self-restraint, is the main cause of the fissures in the progress and natural development of children who are the future of the society. The truncation of the much need love and nurture of the mother, intentionally or otherwise, as she has to do a balancing act in her need to devote quality time to her children and her career demands, is the primary reason for the disruption of the moral fabric of the society.

It is to be noted that a child has an instinctive tendency to learn from the environment, even without direct and rational instruction. This it does by mere observation and imitation in its early life, like the saying, 'Monkey see monkey do'. That the child sometimes behaves in a demanding manner, much to the annoyance of the parents, is its need for the unfulfilled love and attention for which it has the basic desire and which it may feel is missing. Sometimes this neglect is unintentional, yet the offspring is not capable of rationally fathoming its cause, and its only natural reaction is to demand attention, which may be seen as misbehaviour and a negative attitude. This whole misunderstanding of the situation makes the child an unwanted entity.

If both the spouse take lesson from human nature and act according to its laws, marriage can be a life long bed of roses. It is only when the ego takes control and subverts the promptings of natural instinct that the battle for dominance begins and this leads to the destruction of the natural balance. In nature each constituent of a unit has a function that it is made to accomplish. A closer look at the nature of man and women will reveal that they differ in their form, makeup and approach to many things in life. E.g. man seems to attach different importance to sexual endeavors than a woman. His approach would be more of wham, bam, and thank you mam type of relationship. A woman on the other hand would show more delicacy, a long term attitude to relationship and deeper sentimentality. This is perhaps due to the fact that it is she who has to incubate, bear and nurture the result of the sexual relationship. Her attachment with the offspring requires a longer duration of association with it, and so her whole attitude to love itself may be different from a man's. She cannot inculcate the male attitude of shying away from the consequences once the act is over and done with. Now in order to keep the interest of the male alive Nature has endowed the female with attraction and allure to keep him in the circuit. A wife who sees and understands this attribute of nature more wisely will carry out her doings in line with her instincts, and keep her husband charmed and better attached than one who does not. She will try and show understanding of his occasional uncaring behaviour and be more accommodative and forgiving. She will use her other inbuilt charms to keep him in line, like keeping herself made-up and attractive to him, and as it is said that 'the way to a man's heart is through his stomach', by making his favourite dishes from time to time etc. This will tilt the balance in her favour sooner or later. The husband on the other hand should see the nature of a woman in view and allure her with occasional gifts to pamper her. A man has to see the nature of the female and praise for her beauty and give her the assurance of his love from time to time, by exhibiting firmness, yet with politeness. Despite the change in approaches due to the changing times, the basis of nature does not change. What was feminine instinct then is still feminine instinct today, and the same goes for the male. A little knowledge of the nature of humans will go a long way to make the relationship healthy and balanced.

In some eastern societies a marriage may be an arranged affair by the family or a third party, and the spouses may only meet after the formalization of the bond. In most liberated societies however, it is a direct arrangement between the partners. In the direct method the main advantage is the two know each other first hand, right from the time they meet and court. However, in this method the tendency of each is perhaps to subconsciously impress the other by presenting the best impression most of the time. There is also the natural distraction of infatuation to shy away from the real nature of the beloved by mainly looking at the good and pleasing side. One tends to see only what one wants to see. The true nature of each may come to light only after the wedlock and this is where the trouble beings. Perhaps by then it is a little late in the day to make amend. In the arranged marriage one starts off by accepting the spouse for what they are as they are, and the feeling of love begins only after the relationship has been established. This said, there is really no guarantee either way whether the match will last out a lifetime. The desire to sacrifice and readjust to the demands of the situation and to restrain oneself for the common good of the family is the key toward the evolution of the society as a whole, and it is this end which should be kept in mind and be reflected upon from time to time in a difficult situation.

Chapter Six
THE INDOMITABLE TRIAD

A triad or a cycle of three is seen to be a frequently occurring sequence in Nature. Many natural phenomena usually complete in three stages, three parts or three phases, e.g.

1. The triad of *thought*, *word* and *deed* can account for most functions of human activity.

2. Human existence on earth is usually covered by the sequence of *birth*, *life* and *death*.

3. The triad of human evolution is seen in the development of *body*, *mind* and *Soul*.

4. Matter is seen to exist in the three states of *solid*, *liquid* and *gas*.

5. The three phases of life could be represented by *past*, *present* and *future*, or *yesterday*, *today* and *tomorrow*.

6. A day is usually divided into the three stages of *morning*, *noon* and *night*.

The list can go on and on, but let's pause here to reflect on these first.

An examination of the above triad sequence shows that for a fuller understanding of such natural phenomena it is essential to study the three stages or states, both individually and collectively. Though each stage is a complete domain by itself yet it contributes to the entire picture only in combination with the others. Let us study these phenomena in some detail and see if there is any reasonable connection between these stages, and if this exercise makes any viable sense. It may be pointed out at the very outset that this is not a scientific paper and relies heavily on common sense, some conjecture and derived logic. It should be approached with an open mind and seen in the context of what it says rather seeking proof to its refutation.

Thoughts or ideas exist at the meta-physical level and are captured by some activities of chemicals in the brain. Or is it the reverse? I.e. the thoughts impinge on the brain and thus result in the release of chemicals in it, which then transmits signals to its agents, the senses, to define all activity in life? This intricate question, much like the chicken or the egg situation, keeps man probing and guessing for answers from the time he started to think about himself. Now, if chemical activity is the basic cause, then chemicals and how they work are questions for medical experts to decipher, and are best left for them to tackle. But if, the thought is the origination of the process, then speculation and philosophy can try its hands first. However, for the present it is sufficient for us to accept the fact that some process does happen in the brain, and that this is what sets man thinking, planning and then acting.

The intangible '*idea*' or '*thought*' sets in motion some activity in the brain which is responsible to convert the thought to an expressible form through *words*. Words are the intermediary stage of giving vent to feelings, and are instrumental to bring the idea or the abstract to the domain of physical expression. Now, to be able to flourish and achieve material existence, these thoughts, that result in words or plans so to say, have to be acted upon through the performance of physical acts or *deeds*. Only then can they be established or said to have an effect on the material world. In other words, the intangible ideas or thoughts go through a process of expression and planning, and then through action can be made into tangible objects or things. The entire activity, comprising the process of *thoughts, words* and *deeds* goes to accomplish the functions of the triad. This is how the intangible or *meta-physical* gets converted to the *physical* or the material plane of existence. Were a thought or idea not expressible in words or plans it would be very difficult to put it in practice or action. It would then remain an innate or a dormant notion, not able to leave any effect or accomplish any change in the material world. If you bear with the logic and reasoning of this discourse it will try to show that the direction of the effect is in fact really cyclical and has a multidimensional tendency i.e. although the beginning of the exercise of life may have been at the meta-physical level of thought and has ultimately reached the physical state of matter; it can also reverse or traverse the course of conversion from the physical to the original or the meta-physical form, and finally trace a complete cyclical pattern.

It is very difficult to accept a thought or idea to be a reality unless there is some tangible effect on the material world. If the effect can be felt and observed, it can be experimented with and proven or disproved, and its existence becomes either acceptable or is rejected by man. It is in the nature of humans to question, verify and judge, and only then accept or reject the validity of an idea.

A child is a conception of thought, or 'conceiving of an idea to conceive' a child. Once the thought occurs in the mind it is expressed and acted upon, which results in a physical outcome.

Sometimes this entire thought process is consciously understood and knowingly implemented by the conceiving couple, but sometimes the outcome is an unplanned result of the act. This example illuminates the triad of *thought*, *word* and *deed.*

Let us examine another triad, *Birth, life* and *death*.

The start of life at birth is similar to the origination of thought of the previous triad. The beginning of life comes from, and starts with, an unconscious phase in human existence. This contention will become clearer with the following example. A baby may be born possessing, some or all, innate knowledge, but is unable to utilize it to its own advantage because of the child's inability to convert it into coherent action. This form of knowledge is an unconscious manifestation of awareness, and is somehow a *meta-physical* state or form of knowing i.e. it may be in the possession of the child, but he does not yet know how to utilize it or benefit from it *physically*. As life progresses, the child starts to get aware or conscious of its surroundings. It develops hand and eye coordination, and learns to utilize its own faculties. It is in a way slowly *'discovering'* its knowledge; in other words is becoming aware or removing the *'cover'* of what is as yet hidden and not within its conscious grasp.

With the passage of time and the development of its faculties, the child learns, by trial and error at first, and then through experience and intelligence. It then begins to gain awareness and conscious knowledge about the world. The extent to which it will go depends on a number of factors such as environmental, circumstantial, psychological etc. The childhood phase is in reality phase of coming out from *'unconsciousness* to *consciousness'*. It is not essential that each of us will acquire or reach the level of consciousness fully, for most pass on without ever fathoming or harnessing their full potential. Why? This is a separate topic by itself, and shall be dealt with some other time. Now, with the coming of age one seems to achieve full control over one's faculties, and that is when one is said to have grown up. This is the stage when one is aware of, and in control of oneself. This is in fact a state of being *'consciously conscious'*. With a further passage of time human faculties begin to retard and tend to lose full efficiency. In this stage one may be aware or conscious, knowledgeable and even wiser, but on a physical decline, because then he/she is not able to do all that much as could be done in the past. This is the stage when one is '*consciously* becoming *unconscious*'. The drift to final unconsciousness is known as death. Death is a condition when physical faculties stop functioning, yet perhaps awareness and knowledge has taken a full cycle and gone from one unconscious state to another, having traversed an all important in-between stage of 'conscious awareness'. It is not essential that each one of us will acquire or reach this level and most pass on without ever fathoming or harnessing their full potential. Why? This again is a separate topic by itself. So the triad of *life, birth* and *death* is now understandable,

The triad of *body, mind* and *soul* is another interesting phenomenon to examine. The development of the human body, seems to be the outcome of a long and steady evolutionary process and upward progression of matter, which in itself is perhaps a conversion from '*meta-physical*' to '*physical*' or material domain. The Greek philosophers considered all matter to consist of atoms, and that these atoms were the smallest particles which could not be broken down any further. Modern science has come a long way from there and has even smashed the atom down to its elementary particles, which themselves seem neither like particles nor elementary, because they do not exist freely in nature nor seem to be matter at all. They can be conceptualized mathematically and may be computed from their non-physical properties. Elementary particles are seen to be a combination of different forms of energy like electric, magnetic and gravitational. If this is what a human body consists of then it is surely something else besides being matter alone, and, this is a point to ponder and study.

At every stage of life a person is learning, consciously or unconsciously, or as has been said earlier, is discovering his/her innate knowledge. He/she is really grooming oneself for the next stage of existence and is slowly evolving towards it. Death, which is nothing but this stage, if seen this way will be viewed positively rather than feared or mentally avoided. The stage of living through physical and mental life is the process of the molding of the Soul-nurturing or the decaying of it. The Soul is a *cohesive life force*, and it seeps through all living bodies, and is intrinsically integrated with each living single cell of it. It is the most evolved form of life. It is a higher rung of the ladder than mind on the scale of holarchy. (This concept is discussed in detail in the essay 'Evolution the inevitable phenomenon').

The Soul's characteristics can be speculated from the holonic point of view, where it is seen that as the mind transcends and incorporates the holon of the body, the Soul must transcend and incorporate the holon of the mind, and as a consequence all holons before it. Now, studying the characteristics of the mind reveals that it is capable of receiving and processing thoughts and then converting them to words, schemes and actions. The Soul must thus be capable of this and one step more. The increase in the capability of the holon of the Soul gives it the power not only to think but also communicate with other minds, incorporate and transcend them. This may be a questionable concept but none the less a logical next step in terms of holarchy. It gives the Soul a capability to perceive and perhaps act both in this and another dimension -- itself more evolved than the realm of the physical Universe. The Soul must possess the capacity of both singular and a collective awareness, meaning that it can exist in both the physical and the metaphysical phases of existence. Like both the mind and the body can be promoted, developed, and evolved by constructive acts and doings, -- e.g. good food and exercise are necessary for a healthy body; faith, discipline and mental exercise are needed for the mind, -- so also the Soul can be cultivated and nurtured by good acts or moral deeds, but cringed, shrunk or diminished by neglect and a wrong attitude. And as in the act of sieving the coarse grains are rejected, so the same principle of selection can be applied to the process of progressive evolution of any system; be it body, mind or Soul, or any other. The secret of progress of a system is to have knowledge of the process that promotes wellness, and aids the reformation from a coarse or mundane level to evolve to the next stage.

The next triad of *solid, liquid* or *gas* is a study of the states in which matter can exist, depending upon the content of its energy. E.g. water can exist in the form of ice – solid state, as water – liquid state, or as steam—gaseous state. The chemical composition of the three states is the same H_2O (two atoms of hydrogen and one atom of oxygen go to make a molecule of water.) Only its physical outlook changes with the change of state. The primary difference is the amount of energy or latent heat each condition has. To change water into ice one needs to take away heat energy from it to the tune of 80 calories per gram. On the other hand to convert the same water to steam one has to add 540 calories of heat energy to every gram. Energy, once again, an intangible or non-physical entity can in some way be equated with consciousness or awareness as discussed above. The conversion from a pre-born state to take human shape, at the time of birth, must also be an addition of some kind of energy, force or power to the previous level, that which would enable it to withstand the conditions and situations of this material world. The whole process may not be instantaneous but requires a period of nine months of incubation. The living of life through the material mode is akin to going through the process of elevation in the energy content i.e. going from an unconscious mode to awareness and control of one's faculties. When sufficient energy, or as in our discussion above, enough awareness, has been accumulated, a change of state becomes imminent. This change of state in the case of living things is called death. Seen this way, death is nothing but a mode of transference of existence from one state to another. To recollect what has been said above, a human seems to be born in an unconsciously conscious state, out of which it struggles to gain awareness all its life, and then consciously transfers to a 'super' or 'above' conscious mode of existence. This brings us to the next triad of nature.

The triad of *past, present* and *future* is a sequential triad for the passage of time—itself a commodity of trading existence. The purpose of which can not be all 'here and now',—or as it has been said, " Eat, drink and be merry, for tomorrow you die".

As discussed in the essay ' A Muslim's destiny', every *Now* (which is also known as present) was once out *There* (that is also called the future), and will eventually become a *Then* (which is the past); and so the natural cycle of life continues to churn. This is how time is spent, and with it, all human effort. Or to say it another way; -- time and effort seem to recede or deplete. In a way they go back. Now, according to the laws of Physics and so also of Nature – 'to every action there is an equal and opposite reaction'. Hence, if time and every thing connected with it goes in a certain direction, something should come out of it as the 'effect of that cause', and would proceed in the opposite direction. The outcome of this decrease in time, etc. is the increase in knowledge and/ or awareness. In other words there is a price to be paid for every thing. In yet another way, gain in awareness is the return of ones investment of time and effort -- or, 'consummation of the self '. This achievement may not be a monetary gain, but believe me it is worth much more. One thing that comes out of all human activity is the unveiling and expanding of new vistas of vision i.e. the furthering of knowledge and awareness. Every step in physical, mental and spiritual advancement is basically the increase of awareness and knowledge, which consequently leads to 'self-growth' and further evolution. See how beautifully Nature maneuvers the evolution of matter to mind to body and then Soul through its passage of time.

Let us now see the meaning of the triad of *morn, noon* and *night.* The dawn of civilization, the rising of the sun, the fulfillments of life to its optimum capacity, etc. are all symbolic of enlightenment, visibility and awareness and capability. As we have been discussing all along, awareness and knowing is the key to all survival and meaningful existence. Maximum awareness is visible at the prime of life. Most vitality and energy, from the sun, is given out at its peak -- the noon. The day having thus dispensed with its energy, leaves the world in darkness -- the night. This night is really a period of incubation for the entire creation to take in and assimilate the effects of their effort during the day, and, having thus evolved through the cycle of the triad, be set to begin at a new evolved or different level at the start of the next day, all over again. To traverse the path of life from birth to prime and then to death is accomplished, as said earlier, by self-consummation i.e. by spending or utilizing of the available time and energy. This is done either knowingly or unknowingly, during the triad of morn, noon and night. If done knowingly, self-satisfaction can be achieved and higher meaning of life seen and understood, and one is said to have lived a fulfilled and useful life. If done unknowingly, all life is spent at the level of mundane animal's existence, fulfilling the chores of the body and the flesh, neither nourishing the mind nor the Soul. This is akin to being held back in a sieve and not filtering to the next stage of higher evolution.

Natural phenomena show continuity from the beginning to the end, in actuality there seems to be no beginning and no end at all. As said earlier a cyclical pattern is perhaps the order of the day. All the triads studied so far show this behaviour e.g. morning, noon and night is a continuous happening without a visibly clear distinction as to the end of the morning and the beginning of noon, and then the day gradually turns into night without a clear demarcation between the ending of light and the beginning of darkness. Only when a state is well established can we give it a name of a distinct mode of the triad. The rate of change is so gradual that at normal levels of study the discernment is not distinguishable. Even at the macro or the micro scales there is no possibility of any clear picture. Now, on the macro scale i.e. at the stellar level, both distances and time lapses are so large that their immensities are still not grasped by man. Observations and measurements are still being studied in detail to make viable sense. In space, energy and matter frames are limitless, and it is difficult to discern as to where energy dimensions end and matter begins, as they overlap and become indistinguishable. At the other end of scale, at the quantum level, things take on a similar hue and a clear distinction between matter and energy once again becomes hazy.

Quantum mechanics is the scientific study of micro systems i.e. systems at the minute end of the scale. At those levels matter shows dual characteristics i.e. it behaves both as a particle and a wave of energy. This may be a difficult concept to grasp, but is handled explicitly at the mathematical level. Yet to express in terms of communicative language, it can be seen as a concurrence of a simultaneous physical and metaphysical manifestation; meaning that if one tries to measure the momentum and the position of a sub-atomic particle at any given moment, it will not be accurately determinable. If the momentum can be measured with some certainty the particles position will be incoherent, and if the position is clearly ascertained its momentum will not be ascertainable. Consider this truth for a minute and one realizes that at the point of conversion from the meta-physical to the physical, it is neither physical nor meta-physical, and it may be more accurate to say that it is both physical and meta-physical at the same time. However, one derives the inference that at that level both are interchangeable and fluid. Yet the origination seems to be at the meta-physical level, because, that which cannot be ascertained with certainty is more in the realm of 'unknown', and that an 'unknown' is not a physical entity -- at best only some speculation. It must reside at the meta-physical level and then be converted to an entity or a physical state to be tangible or become 'known'. If all action can be broken down to its final rudiments it too will manifest a similar disposition, i.e. before execution an action exists in the mind as a thought, at a meta-physical or an energy level. The interaction of that state with the physical body produces what it produces in the brain. The conversion of this thought then goes through the process of planning or expression through words. These syllables, unless expressed vocally or on paper, remain in the realm of both material and non-material at the same time. Once put into practice they become material and obtain an 'identity of an entity'. They are then governable by the laws of classical Physics. It thus goes to show that all existence is primarily at the meta-physical level, becoming an identifiable material presence by the converting power of the mind; and then having lived through a period in the space--time continuum seem to dissipate into oblivion, yet leaving some effect on the material world of reality and human comprehension.

To quote Asadulla Khan Ghalib, the famous poet philosopher of the East who put this so aptly as:

Hasti kay muth faraib may aajaiyo Asad
Alam tamaam halqa e dam e khayal hai

Be not deceived O Asad,
By the dazzle of creation.

All existence is encircled,
By the net of imagination.

It thus seems that all creation is really a figment of one's imagination. *Whose*? Who can say?

Chapter Seven
THE TWO SIDES OF NATURE

I t may be pointed out at the very outset that this is not a scientific paper and relies heavily on common sense, derived logic and some conjecture. It should be approached with an open mind and seen in the context of what it is trying to say, rather than seeking proof for its refutation.

Nature seems to manifest itself in two states—the 'Physical' and the 'Metaphysical'. The Physical form consists of all material existence, both visible and invisible. This phase is identifiable through the five human senses of, Touch, Taste, Sight, Smell and Hearing. The Metaphysical phase of Nature, however, on the other hand, covers all forms that may be beyond common comprehension, for example things like the energy content of the Universe, forces like gravity and even phenomena like the psychology of the Kosmos -- (this is different from the *Cosmos* , better explained in books on holonic theory. Briefly, it is the cumulative manifestation of all matter, energy and even psychology of the Universe.), Human sense can, in some cases, be developed to a different dimension, called the sixth sense. This sense gives one the capacity to tap into the realm of the Metaphysical and fathom certain superhuman phenomena.

A closer examination of the two phases reveals that, it is really the Metaphysical mode of Nature that permeates all aspects of '*thought*', '*word*' and '*deed*' -- the triad of human existence, and that the coordinated manifestation of the three results in the making of a human being.

'Energy' and 'Matter' are related and interchangeable as per Einstein's famous equation: $E=mC^2$. The equation is an epoch of human thought. It explains and enhances the understanding of the hitherto unquestionable concept of the indestructibility of matter. Now matter and energy are understood to be interchangeable. Matter can be thought of and explainable as ' rest ', or ' dormant energy'. It takes a large of amount of energy to be ' condensed' or 'dormanted' to convert to a small amount of matter; whereas the destruction of a small amount of matter can result in the release of a large amount of energy. The process of creation of energy by the transformation of the mass of matter has been adequately demonstrated through various experiments. The atomic explosion is the most common example -- where the destruction of a small amount of matter can result in the creation of an immense amount of energy. Having grasped the idea and the relation between the interchangeability of matter and energy, it comes to mind to study the relationship of another interesting phenomenon, that of ' thought' or 'idea', and ' energy', and their correlation.

Thought too, like matter seems to be some form of energy-related process and/ or a manifestation of it in another domain, and like matter it may also be dormant or rest energy in a realm of its own, different from the physical world.

Now, if energy and matter are equitable as per $E=mc^2$, then 'thought' may also be equitable to 'energy' and vice versa in a similar form. Perhaps as T= E k. Where T stands for 'thought', E for 'energy' and ' k' would be a constant or an equating factor.

To fulfill any 'idea' or 'thought' , it has to be brought from the realm of the meta-physical and be expressed as words or plans. This plan has then to be acted upon in the physical world in order to produce some effect on the senses. But to act one requires energy. Where does this energy come from? It seems to take birth due to a similar process as that of the convertibility of the energy to matter. In the net analysis it is the thought (meta-physical) which when harnessed consciously, converts to the domain of words or plan, and when that plan is acted upon finally gets transferred into a material existence. Physical world thus seems to be the end result of the metaphysical thought or idea. Now, to fully appreciate the equation we have to understand the function of the term 'k'. This seems to be nothing more than the ' level of intensity' or the gravity of the 'desire' i.e. the greater the demand or need, the higher the quest, and deeper the thought. Resulting in the overflow of energy from the Cosmic reservoir, which then leads to the level of effort needed to convert into a physical form. Now thought, that seems to reside in the tranquil world of the unconscious has to be first brought out of its slumber of undisturbed existence, and made understandable by bringing it to the mode of consciousness. How this happens is still a subject of both philosophic and scientific research.

As just said, Science has shown that according to the laws of the conservation of energy and matter, the physical and the metaphysical phases are interlinked, and that they can be generated one from the other. If matter (the Physical entity) is a derivative of energy which is the metaphysical content of the Kosmos, then the physical state is really the conversion or transformation of that metaphysical. It is then perhaps the metaphysical alone, that may be required for the existence of the entire Kosmotic system, and seems to be its sole originator. Astrophysicists observe that the Metaphysical or non-physical content of the Universe is far greater than its physical, and if empty space is also taken into account and considered to be some form of Metaphysics, then the existence of the ' physical part' is reduced to a very small portion in the entire universe. Remember the saying that, " … it is the mind over matter … ", for is it not the mind (the metaphysical), that conceives, and the body (the physical) that acts or implements the idea? So Metaphysics or the non-material seems to be the principal ingredient of all Natural phenomena – originating at the metaphysical level and reaching a completion at the physical. This is perhaps due to the fact that the thought or idea is in the 'free state of energy' when in the unconscious, and it is light and free to move in any of the three directions at any given moment, much like matter when in the gaseous state; Or so to say, as water when in the form of steam. The conscious redirection of the 'content' of thought, in the process of its conversion to word or plan, seems to reduce its freedom of movement and its fluidity from three directions to two. This is like the case of water when condensed from steam. Where, steam has the freedom to move in all three directions at a time but as water it is restricted to two. A further transformation of word or plan to action in the physical world is akin to the change of state from liquid to solid. For a solid is nothing but the 'fixation' of the liquid state. This reduces its movement to a single direction at any given moment of time. This just goes to show that the change in energy brings about changes in the nature of freedom and /or ability of the entity. However, it is interesting to note that once the physical state begins to accumulate upon itself it gains the capacity to coalesce and intensify its property of attraction. This it does by virtue of the strength of the force of gravity. So much so, that if matter can become a 'black hole', a highly dense form of matter, where not even light energy can escape from its grip.

Thoughts or ideas exist at the meta-physical level and originate from the activities of chemicals in the brain. Or is it the reverse? i.e. the impingement of thoughts on the brain result in the release of chemicals in it, which then transmit signals to its agents, the senses, to promote activity in life? This intricate question, much like the chicken or the egg situation, has kept man probing and guessing for answers from the time he started to think about himself. Now, if chemical activity is the basic cause, then chemicals and how they work are questions for chemists and medical experts to decipher and are best left for them to tackle. But if, the thought is the origination of the process, then speculation and philosophy can try its hands first. However, for the present it is sufficient for us to accept the fact that some process does happen in the brain, and that this is what keeps man alive – thinking, planning and acting.

One idea that emerges from recent scientific experiments is the fact that to neuroscientists, learning is a biological process in which the connections—or synapses—among the brain nerve cells becomes stronger. That means processed information leaves a physical trace within the structure of the brain. The more often the connection is activated, the stronger it becomes, making us smarter. The working of the synapses and the conversion of the metaphysical through to the physical is still not clear knowledge. However the metaphysical thought does seem to have an interaction with the physical through these synapses.

- A synapse is the small gap between two neurons, where nerve impulses are relayed by a neurotransmitter from the axon of a presynaptic (sending) neuron to the dendrite of a postsynaptic (receiving) neuron. It is referred to as the synaptic cleft or synaptic gap.
- During synaptic transmission, the action potential (an electrical impulse) triggers the synaptic vesicles of the pre-synaptic neuron to release neurotransmitters (a chemical message).
- These neurotransmitters diffuse across the synaptic cleft (the gap between the pre and post-synaptic neurons) and bind to

specialized receptor sites on the post-synaptic neuron.

- If the neurotransmitter is excitatory (eg. noradrenaline) then the post-synaptic neuron is more likely to fire an impulse. If the neurotransmitter is inhibitory (eg. serotonin) then the post-synaptic neuron is less likely to fire an impulse.

- The excitatory and inhibitory influences are summed to determine whether/how frequently the neuron will fire (summation). At the dendrites, the chemical message is converted back into an electrical impulse and the process of transmission occurs again.

The intangible 'idea' or 'thought' sets in motion some activity in the brain. This is responsible to convert the thought to an expressible form through 'words' or 'plans'. Words are the intermediary stage of giving vent to feelings, and are instrumental to bring the idea, or the abstract to the domain of physical existence. Now, to be able to flourish and achieve material being, these *'ideas or thoughts'*, that result in *'words or plans'*, have to be acted upon through the performance of *'acts or deeds'*. They can then be established or said to have an effect on the material world,-- recognizable by the senses. In other words, the intangible ideas or thoughts have to go through a process of expression and planning, and then through action can be made into tangible objects or things. The entire activity, comprising the process of thoughts, words and deeds goes to accomplish the functions of the triad. And as said earlier, that though each is a complete domain in itself, yet have to act in conjunction with the others to complete the picture. Were a thought or idea not expressible in words or plans, it would be very difficult to put it in practice and action. It would then remain an innate or a dormant notion, not able to leave any effect, or accomplish change in the material world; or perhaps be instinctive acts geared to realizing the effect unconsciously, as is seen in the case of lower forms of life.

It is in the nature of humans to question, verify and judge, and only then accept or reject the validity of an idea. If the effect of a thing can be felt and observed it can be experimented with and then proven or disproved. Now the difficulty of experimentally proving the relationship of thought and energy is due to the fact that both are metaphysical entities, existing in a non physical realm, and thus unverifiable by direct physical experiments. Their correlation can perhaps be observed by their effect on say, the reactions of a person or his psychological behaviour, and thus inferred through some indirect experiments. Let us take an example here. A child is a conception of thought, or 'manifestation of an idea to conceive' an offspring. Once the thought occurs in the mind, it is expressed and acted upon to get an effect. Sometimes this entire thought process is consciously understood and knowingly implemented by the conceiving couple, but sometimes the outcome is the involuntary result of the act, much like the instinctive behaviour of animals. Thoughts have to be shown the light of the day by putting them through a plan and action. In any case a 'reaction' is the result of some 'action' and could not have come about in isolation, one of the other. The action performed on thought is the ' cause' or stimulus, the ' effect' or 'outcome' of which is the material form that comes forth, and it is this form which leaves its effects on the senses.

In the human system, the conversion from a pre-born state to human shape, at birth, must also be an addition or manipulation of some kind of energy, force or power of the previous level. There also must be a pre –birth stage which is the fluid state of energy with the capability to traverse any direction freely. This is the stage or level of idea or thought alone, as seen above a state of energy, capable of free movement in any of the three directions. A further conversion or the implementation of this thought or idea, through the expression or plan, takes a direction of restricting the movement or fluidity from the three to two dimensions. The form of the formation of the fetus is the physical manifestation of the idea or thought having traversed through planning to the action phase. The process results in the evolution of the energy from complete freedom of movement in the three, to two and finally the single direction of existence. This transformation of energy or the evolution of it would enable it to withstand the conditions of this material world, and also to bear the rigors of independent existence. The whole process does not seem to be instantaneous but requires a period of many months of incubation-- where the energy coupled with other metaphysical forces of human psychology rear up the body material, in the melting pot of the womb, to a human level of independent self-existence . The living of life through the material mode is akin to going through the process of change, or some form of further readjustment in the energy content i.e. going from an unconscious mode, which may require low kinetic energy, to awareness, which may need more kinetic energy to remain vigilant and be able to act. When sufficient energy, or as in our discussion above, enough knowledge and awareness has been accumulated by the physical phase, and that which has left some effect on the world during its span of existence here, another change of state becomes imminent. This change of state in the case of living things is called death. Seen this way, death is nothing but a mode of transference of existence from one state to another. To recollect what has been said above, a human seems to be born in an unconscious or unaware state, out of which it struggles to gain knowledge and awareness all its life. This it may do either consciously or otherwise. But having traversed this phase it transfers to a 'super' or 'above' the physical state of living to some other form of existence. Seen this way the whole triad of *birth, life* and *death* takes on a new meaning, and death then comes to be seen as a form of transference from one form of living to another and not an annihilation of existence altogether.

The dawn of civilization, the rising of the sun, the attainment of life to its optimum capacity, etc. are symbolic of enlightenment, vitality and awareness of capability. As we have been discussing all along, awareness and knowledge is the key to all survival and meaningful existence. Maximum strength is visible at the prime of life. Most vitality and energy from the sun is gained at its peak – the noon hour. The day having dispensed with its energy leaves the world in darkness—the night. This night is really a period of incubation for the entire creation to take in and assimilate the effects of the causes of the day, and having gone through the cycle of the triad of morning, noon and night, be set to begin at a different level at the start of the next day. The passage of the entire creation or the 'Kosmos' through the period of a given day adds to it something extra, enhances or evolves it in some form either consciously or unconsciously, and raises its level in some way and perhaps makes it more valuable. To elaborate the idea further let us see the change that has taken place in the life of man himself. He started as an uncivilized cave dweller and gradually evolved to the level of being able to build skyscrapers and live in them. All along the period of this change he acquired more knowledge and awareness of the world and surely became more capable, and perhaps added more value to his own capabilities with the passage of time. To traverse the path of life from birth to prime and then to death is to accomplish, as seen elsewhere, the act of self-consummation i.e. knowingly or unknowingly, spending or utilizing the time and energy, available during a lifetime, in the pursuit of awareness and knowledge. This gain in awareness and or knowledge is in reality the acquisition of some form of vitality, or so to say fruitful use of the available 'manna'. If this is done knowingly, self-satisfaction can be achieved and a higher meaning of life can be seen and understood, and one is said to have lived a fulfilled life. If on the other hand this is done unknowingly, all life is spent at the level of mundane animal existence, not elevating the mind or the soul. This is akin to being held back in the sieve or the grader of life and not be filtered to the next level of conscious progress.

One thing that comes out of all human activity is the unveiling and expanding of new vistas of vision, the furthering of awareness and increase of knowledge, which are surely the prime tools for progress, and when properly utilized lead to self-growth and conscious evolution. See how beautifully Nature maneuvers and evolves the unconscious non-material metaphysical existence through the passage of time and energy , first to the holon of the *body*, then the *mind* and eventually the *soul*.

One learns at every stage of life. The process of learning can, however, be conscious or unconscious, and as has been said, this process of discovering is in fact an act of 'removing the cover' from over one's own innate or hidden knowledge. One is really grooming oneself for the next stage of existence, and is slowly evolving towards it. Death is nothing but this next stage of human evolution. Seen this way death comes to be viewed positively, rather than feared or mentally avoided. Further, this concept of the triad of birth, life and death may be an evolution of the very thought itself over the existentialist's belief -- that with death comes the end of life and all existence. The stage of living through physical and mental life is the process of the molding of the Soul -- nurturing or the decaying of it, as has been said earlier, through positive or negative actions of the body. The Soul, which is a *'cohesive life force'*, may be an offshoot of the *'Universal Cosmic Force'* and seeps through all living bodies. It is intrinsically integrated with each living cell of it. It is an evolved form of life and it is at a higher rung of the ladder than the holon of the mind on the scale of holarchy. Therefore, it is perhaps not for the mind to fathom the soul, but the soul can understand and encompass the mind. The Soul's characteristics can be speculated from the holonic theory, where it is seen that, as the mind transcends and incorporates the holon of the body, the Soul must transcend and incorporate the holon of the mind and as a consequence all holons before it. Now, studying the characteristics of the mind reveals that it is capable of receiving and processing thoughts through its interaction with the brain, and then converting them to words and schemes for actions. The Soul must thus be capable of this and one step more. The increase in the capability of the holon of the Soul would give it the power not only to think but also communicate with other minds. This may be a questionable concept but is none- the- less a logical follow through as the next step in terms of holarchy. Extrapolating further, the Soul would have a capability to perceive and perhaps act in the realm of this world as well as the next dimension of existence. This dimension itself may be more evolved than the realm of the physical Universe. The Soul would possess the capacity of both a singular and a collective awareness, meaning that it can exist in the physical, as individual entities, and also the metaphysical phase where it can manifest a collective existence. Like both the mind and the body it can be promoted, developed, and evolved as just said, by constructive acts and doings, as has been said earlier i.e. as good food and exercise are necessary for a healthy body; faith, discipline and mental exercise are needed for the mind, and so healthy deeds and a positive attitude would be the food for the development of the soul.

We have seen that in the act of sieving the coarse grains are rejected and held back, and the purer or finer material passes through. The fineness of the material is really its improvement or evolution to pass through to the next higher level of abode. The same principle of selection is applicable in the progress of a self-evolving system. The system of body, mind or Soul, or any other, where fineness and purity are desired, must also follow the same principle. The secret of progress of a self-developing system is its inbuilt capacity to use the method or process that promotes wellness, which aids in its reformation from a coarse or lower level to evolve to the next higher stage.

Natural phenomena show continuity from the beginning to the end. In actuality there seems to be no beginning and no end at all. As said earlier a cyclical pattern is perhaps the way Nature operates. However, each successive cycle is instrumental in enhancing the process of evolution of Self. All the triads studied so far show this behaviour, e.g. morning, noon and night is a continuous happening without a visibly clear distinction as to the end of the morning and the beginning of noon, and then the day gradually turns into night without a clear demarcation between the ending of light and the onset of darkness. Only when a mode of a triad is well established, can we name it as a distinctive state. This rate of change is so gradual that at normal levels of study the discernment is not possible. This process of the phenomenon is true both at the macro or the micro scales, and there seems no possibility of a clear picture. Now, on the macro scale i.e. at the stellar level, both distances and time lapses are so large that man is not able to grasp their immensities and perhaps thus misses the point of change or demarcation. Observations and measurements are still being studied in detail to make viable sense. In space, energy and matter frames are limitless, and it is difficult to discern as to where energy dimensions end and matter begins because they overlap and become indistinguishable. At the other end of the scale, at the quantum level, things take on a similar hue and a clear distinction between matter and energy once again becomes hazy. It is however interesting to note that the performance of repeated cycles of the triad holds the secret of its own evolution. This repetition is the basis by which the inherent evolution comes to the surface in some mysterious and magical way, perhaps not yet rationally fathomable.

Quantum mechanics is the science for the study of micro systems i.e. systems at the minute end of the scale. At those levels matter shows dual characteristics i.e. it behaves both as a particle and a wave of energy. This may be a difficult concept to grasp, and it is more clearly fathomable only at the mathematical level. To express in terms of communicative language, it can be seen as a concurrence of a simultaneous physical and metaphysical manifestation. Meaning that, according to Heizenberg's principle of uncertainty, if the momentum of a sub-atomic particle can be measured with some certainty then the particles position will be incoherent, and if the position is clearly determined its momentum will not be accurately ascertained, and that if one tries to simultaneously measure the momentum and the position of a sub-atomic particle they may not be accurately determined. For, On consideration of this truth for a minute one realizes that at the stage of sub-atomic particles there is perhaps an overlap of the meta-physical and the physical, a particle at that level is neither physical nor meta-physical. It may be accurate to say that the object is perhaps, in both the physical and meta-physical condition simultaneously. However one derives the inference that at that stage both states or phases are interchangeable and fluid. Yet, the origination seems to have been at the meta-physical level, because, " that which cannot be ascertained with certainty is more in the realm of the 'unknown' than the ' known', and that an ' unknown' is not a physical entity-- at best some form of speculation ". The 'idea' must thus reside at the meta-physical level and then be converted to an entity or a physical state to become tangible or become 'known'. If all action can be broken down to its final rudiments, it too will manifest a similar disposition, i.e. before execution, an action exists in the mind as an idea, at a meta-physical or pure energy level. The interaction of that state with the physical body, the brain, produces some affect in it, giving rise to consciousness. This consciousness of the thought then takes it through the process of planning or expression through words, into actions. These syllables of words, unless expressed vocally or on paper, remain in the realm of both material and non-material at the same time, as if in a quantum state. Once put into practice they become material and obtain an 'identity of an entity'. They are then governable by the laws of classical Sciences. It thus goes to show that all existence is primarily in the meta-physical plane, becoming an identifiable material presence by the converting process of the 'brain-mind' combination; and then having lived through a period in the 'space-time continuum', seem to dissipate into oblivion, yet leaving some effect on the material world of reality and human comprehension. *The human comprehension itself seem to be nothing but an infinitesimal extension of the Cosmic awareness of Nature of Itself.* This concept and its repercussions have been discussed in more detail in the essay 'The nature of a Natural Deity'.

Energy and matter, as seen earlier, are both related and interchangeable as per Einstein's epochal formula. To complete any 'idea' or 'thought' it has to be brought from the realm of the meta-physical and energized, and then acted upon in the realm of the physical. Now to act one requires energy. Where does this energy come from? It seems to take birth due to the convertibility of thought, akin to the release of energy in the process of energy and matter inter-conversion as per Einstein. In the net analysis it is the 'thought' (meta-physical) which is perhaps some form of latent, hidden or untapped energy, and which finally gets converted into action, a (physical) manifestation of it, having been brought to the conscious and a viable state, after passing through the process of planning. In the essay 'Philosophic thought – secular and religious', we have discussed this concept a little further, but suffice it to reflect here that, According to Aristotle, "forms and 'ideas' are not outside matter. The forms don't change but matter can. The acorn – in form is the same – but matter can change from acorn to tree to furniture, acquiring a different from as it changes. Matter changes and seeks to realize different forms – an acorn seeks to realize the form of an oak tree. A seed seeks to realize the form of a rose. Matter is thus, taking on, striving to realize forms". Reflecting upon this and extrapolating the idea further, it may well be that man is seeking to realize its coveted form – God Itself.

Asadulla Khan Ghalib, the famous poet philosopher of the East makes a very profound observation when he says:

Na tha kutch to Khuda tha
Kutch na hoota to Khuda hoota
Duboya mujh ko honay nay
na hoota main to Kaya hoota?

When naught existed God existed,
Had none there been, God would be.
My own existence lowered me.
Would I not be, what would it be?

The meaning that oozes out from the above verse is that Ghalib, like Plato and Pythagoras, projects the idea that man is fallen divinity. Had he not been brought forth he would have existed at the level of the Deity Itself.

In the end I would like to leave the questioning mind with my question for Ghalib lovers to ponder, decipher accept or reject. Now, if and when I meet Ghalib I will ask him as to why he did not write thus:

Na tha kutch to Khuda tha,

Kutch na hoota to Khuda hoota
-Sujhaya- mujh ko honay nay,
na hota main to Kaya hoota?

When naught existed God existed,
Had none there been, God would be.
My very being, this made me see.
Would I not be, what would it be?

For, if I had not been brought forth I would no doubt have been part of the whole; but an insensitive, unconscious, ignorant part. My very being and individual existence gives me an identity of an entity, and is responsible for making me aware of that fact. Hence perhaps it may be said that the form 'God' is seeking to realize Itself through the material manifestation of passing through the state of matter in the shape of 'man'; and man in his eternal quest is seeking to realize his true essence – *the Spirit* .

Chapter Eight

MUTUAL INFLUENCE OF THE CREATOR AND THE CREATED

Upon observing the Universe closely, one sees some underlying patterns and standard principles on which the entire creation is based and under which the whole of the *Natural system* operates. There is also an interconnection between various 'happenings or events', because without continuity and connection the creation cannot function as a whole. Although some events may seem to take place or exist in isolation yet in reality there is some or the other form of connection that exists in the whole scenario. If there were no connection the whole system would remain fragmented, incomplete and tumble with a breakdown in its communication. To substantiate the idea one only needs to reflect on one's own life. It is lived in three time zones of yesterday, today and tomorrow, or, the past, present and future. All the tree phases are interconnected, for the happenings of the past play a role in shaping the present, and the doings in the present lead the way to the future. Continuity is an essential part of most natural phenomena and an interconnection between them is a prerequisite of the 'wholeness' of the entire system. A system cannot be whole if it is not a sum of its parts, and perhaps more.

The laws of 'cause and effect' are the most basic laws in the Kosmos,

(The word is taken from concept developed in the theory of Holarchy, where it stands to mean the physical Cosmos and all the metaphysical forces within it and also their mutual interplay). These laws are the unifying principle of different phenomena in nature. These phenomena may seem independent and self-contained but are, somehow interconnected and influence one another. The cause and its effect may not necessarily all be in the same frame of reference and hence sometimes incomprehensible at a given point in time and space. Also, there may be a different period of gestation or incubation for different events, though their causes may be similar. Further, as seen in the essay ' The two sides of Nature', the physical act is essentially an off shoot or conversion of the metaphysical thought or word, and when it converts to a material existence it imparts an effect. This effect may either be in the realm of metaphysics or physics. The actions of the body affect the thoughts and vice versa. The end effect may not necessarily be discernable by the senses. What appears to happen at this spot may have its affect at some other juncture and vice versa.

Let us look at some examples to clarify the concept and statements just made. Most things are made up of constituents or building blocks. Even in disarray there is an eventual connection of some sort between them. Continuity is a prerequisite of all events and is essential for evolution. Since the Kosmos is one unit and is also evolving as a whole it is bound to be continuous and connected in one way or the other. Consciousness is the key to this connection and all things are inter-related and inter-connected in the realm of 'Cosmic Consciousness'. To remain connected some method of communication must exist between different parts of the Kosmos, and this communication is the key of control. Without communication no knowledge of the 'Parts' would be available to the 'Whole', and subsequently no information could be transferred from one to the other. Now, the exposure, awareness or knowledge of every individual part results in the 'effect' being passed on and back to the ' Data Bank' of the Kosmos, which holds the sum total of all knowledge and awareness of everything, living or non living, from eternity to the present. Let us take an example to fully appreciate the meaning of this. Take some masons building a wall using bricks. At the initial level they have an idea or a plan to build the wall by placing a number of bricks side by side to make a base. Once this is done they start to raise it by adding successive blocks one over the other. Following the pattern over and over a wall gets erected. Now one of the masons thinks of doing something new to the design of the wall. He starts to build another wall by putting one brick straight and the two sideways on top it. When this wall is completed it has a different arrangement of bricks and a different pattern from the first. The 'data bank' of brick laying has now been enriched by two designs instead of one. A third mason starts his wall by leaving a little space between bricks to allow air to pass through. This becomes another way of raising a wall. This is a typical example of evolution in wall making. With every innovation and creative design the wall making pattern gets enriched and diversified. Once the wall making cyclopedia has evolved, the later generation of masons can always refer to it for any wall making designs. They then move the idea forward, perhaps by making two adjacent walls and putting a roof over them. This is now the beginning of room making. Further along the line comes the building of a house, and the whole field of architecture begins to take shape. When housing becomes a common thing the pattern of living also changes, from the open into the covered comforts of one's own space. This change has its subsequent effect on 'mind', 'body' and 'soul' of people. And the whole attitude has its own impact on the thought and action of subsequent generations, who having learnt from the experiences of their ancestors can innovate and evolve new methods and ideas of their own. It is worth mentioning that all knowledge and information lies within, in the subconscious so to say. It has to be laboriously dug up and brought to the conscious level, to be utilized for the fulfillment of the actor. Every bit of information adds up and the 'Universal Data Bank' begins to grow. The increase in information results in the increase in computation of this data, and with the computation of the data comes about the increase of knowledge. The processing of knowledge eventually adds to increased awareness and consciousness of the entire Kosmotic system.

A teacher—pupil relationship is a two way street, especially in the higher classes. The two interact on a give and take basis. The ideas the teacher imparts attract the student's attention and motivates him to think and then subsequently to act on his own. The student who thinks, questions, and it is then for the teacher, with his greater experience and more profound wisdom, to clarify the pupils thoughts and give them a direction. In this process of interaction the teacher him/herself reflects and sees things from a new angle, that of the student's, thus re-examining his/her own concept of the subject, perhaps getting a few fresh ideas for himself. As long as the relationship is based on the honesty of purpose—that of teaching, learning, seeking and finding, all effort is positive and progressive; but if doubt and deception seeps in, both the teacher and the student become the losers. The real aim of any good education is to develop the society, both the teacher and the student, through this mutual exchange of ideas, to tackle problems and hurdles together and from different angles, and thus be in a position to solve new problems. One to one, each one tries to further the frontiers of knowledge, for, what the student thinks the teacher must think further and vice versa. This forward movement results in growth and progress for both, and an eventual evolution of the system as a whole. Both the student and the teacher progress as a result of the mutual processing of knowledge.

So we see that that every act of man is somehow the cause or the source of another act, and that all causes and effects are inter-related in one way or another, adding to the buildup of consciousness and awareness of the Universe as a whole. Man is thus affecting and is in turn being affected by the happenings of the world and beyond. Each individual's actions may have only an infinitesimal and perhaps unobservable effect on the whole system, yet each single drop goes to make the ocean. While the drop itself achieves fulfillment by merging into it, the ocean too gets richer none the less.

The human mind seems to function incessantly. It does so either at a conscious or an unconscious level, continuously processing information all the time. When it is not functioning in the conscious mode, it is never-the-less working at the sub or unconscious level. The source of knowledge for every mind seems to be the all pervading 'Cosmic Awareness' or 'Cosmic Source', and is the seat of all information. Every mind remains connected with this 'Source' of information all the time, consciously or unconsciously. The connection is in a rather subtle manner, and its functioning goes undetected by the common human senses, which are only adequate for the everyday survival and living. The cosmic connection requires the inculcation of supra or over and above comprehension which develops with evolution of the Self, and perhaps the connection is at a metaphysical level. In other words this 'Cosmic Data Bank' is much like the information available on the 'internet', which is all pervading and is ever present 'out there', in cyber space. This resource and its content can be thought of as a computer. The quantity that can be drawn from the source depends on the strength and capacity of the hardware, also the knowledge of the user to maneuver the computer and the strength of the program to decipher the language of the transmission. The Cosmic phenomenon of consciousness operates in a rather subtle manner, sometimes on a sub, and sometimes at a super human frequency, both of which are perhaps beyond the physical rational mode. Each and every human is, however, connected with it. A human's connection with it, at birth, is at an unconscious level. When it is said that ' the mind develops with age', what is really meant perhaps is, that the development is really taking place of the computing system as a whole. Both at the level of the functioning of the brain, the hardware, and at the developmental level of the software, which starts to decipher the message of this Cosmic information more rationally, at a conscious level. It is interesting to note that in humans the hardware and the software are one and not two separate entities, as is the case with present day computers. As age and sense start taking hold, slowly and gradually, the brain acquires the potential to harness the vibes in space and convert them from subconscious modes of the messages into comprehensible code of language and expression that is understandable by man. Now, with training and development the brain can be made to process even those wavelengths of the 'Cosmic transmission' that are ordinarily beyond normal human grasp. This form of communication has been named as *revelation or inspiration*. This, in other words is the increase in the capacity of the brain and its own evolution to be able to bring extraordinary thoughts and ideas to the fathomable level of awareness and rational understanding, achieved by elevated individuals.

Now, knowledge and awareness are antagonistic to instinct and impulse. The former work at the conscious level and the later at subconscious planes. The more one knows the more aware one becomes, and this growth of awareness and knowledge have a tendency to inhabit basic instinctive behaviour. The two are like two sides of a coin where only one side is visible at any given moment. If the coin is slowly rotated on its edge, one side of it gradually disappears and the other starts to come in view. Knowledge is power, and the more power one gains over one's Self the more ability one acquires, and consequently the more independent one becomes. And, the more independent one feels, the more freedom one gets. This freedom is acquired from the direct controls of 'Mother Nature'. It actually means that with our increase in knowledge and awareness, *Nature* Itself loosens *It's* grip over us and gives us more freedom to manage our own affairs independently, however, within the confines of *It's* laws. This It (Mother Nature) does in a way similar to what parents do with their offspring. The more the grownup's confidence grows in the child's ability, the less supervision is exercised. For, in a child, the growth of ability is none other than the increase in knowledge, awareness and the means to manipulate themselves independently. This continues to advance the ability to manage him/herself using the knowledge and awareness acquired from childhood. Instincts are basically Nature's means of direct control over the creation. It continues communicating the commands at a sub or super conscious level, and then has them implemented through the control of behaviour. Now, knowledge and awareness is the outcome of one's conscious effort in utilizing time and energy, the abundantly available, yet an individually allocated resource of nature. This conscious effort of expending time and energy is in a way the *'consummation of oneself'*, because when time and energy are used up one has consumed them and spent one's own force in the pursuit of a desire. Observed closely, Nature is a 'living, eternal, self subsisting and an ever-sustaining system', yet It places Its own- Self subservient to Its own laws, and does not seem to act outside their boundaries. Sensible men who begin to fathom this quality of Nature begin to emulate it and so gain in wisdom and self amelioration. The dawning of the attributes of Nature on man leads to his evolution towards the nature of Nature Itself, and this is when the pupil get in synchronization with the teacher and vice versa. This is perhaps like the relationship of Phd students and their supervisors, where both student and teacher are pursuing the goal of a completely, hitherto unknown phenomena.

The real achievement of thought is its conversion to deed through action, or in other words the conversion of the metaphysical into the physical. Fulfillment is only achieved when a thought is acted upon. *'Mother Nature' Itself may have got an idea or a thought, but It achieved fulfillment only after accomplishing the act of Creation. If the whole concept had remained just in the form of an idea or thought, 'Nature' would not have achieved any satisfaction or self-fulfillment. Thus the completion or consummation of the 'metaphysical' is, in its being transformed into the 'physical'. i.e. Until the metaphysical does not acquire a material form it remains incomplete or unfulfilled.* Also the reverse is true, that is, that the material human form too is seeking to attain the metaphysical stage by retracing the path of reversal to it. That means that humans are engaged in reverse engineering themselves. Once the physical has come into being the cycle starts to reverse i.e. the 'physical' having gone through evolution and progress, starts the return journey to the 'metaphysical'; Only this time it goes back to the, hitherto unknown or unconscious, with awareness, and having achieved enlightenment and achievement of the purpose for which it was created, and thus the fulfillment of the ' Self'.

Religious thought has slowly dawned, matured and progressively developed from polytheism to monotheism. And then the chronological development of various monotheistic religions show the nurturing and improvement of the human intellect itself with the passage of time. This is reflected in the progress of the method and terminology of the religious messages and revelations as they came to us through successive prophetic utterances and deliveries. The early religious thought dealt with basics and simplicities of life and the narrations were simple episodes of every day happenings which could be grasped by the common man and his nascent mind. That these narratives had deeper significance was fathomed only by later, more developed intellects. That growth in human thinking and the development of human thought is progressive is seen in how the divine message was gradually and successively raised in standard and content from messenger to following messenger. Noah, one of the earlier prophets of monotheism is like an educator and preacher of humanity in its initial stage or, for example, the teacher when humans were in grade I of humanism. The lesson he gave was to inculcate *faith and belief,* without which not much can be achieved. Noah's selected few of each species bred succeeding generations who then became the raw material for the next level of education. And successive prophets and teachers kept up the vigil and continued the process of education by bringing and conveying the messages through revelations from time to time. Somewhere down the line came another icon, Abraham, teacher of higher grades; perhaps II, III and IV. and above. Abraham stepped in as the propagator of the next higher concept. While reinforcing the message of monotheism he expanded it to the next elevation of progress in belief; the lesson of *self- sacrifice.* Continuing further, came Moses, much like a teacher to the finishing school. His message included the ones that had come before, and as an addition and further uplift of humankind he revealed the *basic commandments* and the fundamentals of universal morality. Notice how the message and human education is unfolded keeping in pace with the time and age and the level of human comprehension. The content and complexity of the process can be appreciated by going into the teaching of each one of these reformers. Jesus, came as the teacher of the graduation class, reaffirming all previous teachings and adding *love and compassion* to the curriculum. All teachings were harmonious and the education of humanity had progressed towards the culmination of its course. The barbarous uncouth man had come a long way from the cave. However, some fine tuning had to be done and that he had to be guided to lead an independent life, armed with the implements to do so. The final message was a sum total of all previous teachings and it seemed a final degree was to be awarded in man's educational upbringing. Muhammad was sent to refresh the lessons of the past classes and to confer the post-graduation degree. He should be seen as a teacher of the last semester in which man is taught to educate himself with the lessons imparted by all the previous teachers at his disposal and the book of reference brought by him. The final message's central theme is *balance and justice* based on the laws of *Cause* and *effect.* As in our example of education so in real life, no teacher and degree is essential after the Masters has been awarded. That any further acquisitions of Phds. and the like are primarily the outcome of self education and research. Having got the education through the various scholars and the book of reference one now has the tools and implements for self-improvement and uplift. If the lesson or the message is not comprehended or well understood one cannot blame the teacher or the book. One has to make a concerted and redirected effort to grasp and understand it.

The above example of religious education and the transformation of human thought with the passage of time and age is applicable to various modes of natural human evolution and transformation. Here 'Nature' is the teacher and humans are the 'pupil'. Observed closely the ' Creator – created' relationship is also based on a principle of exchange. Whether the Creator created everything for some predetermined purpose or to leave it to evolve on its own is a subject of eternal debate. Yet, the Creator, none the less, imparted to the creation, certain qualities that enable and assist it to strive through life. In this process of striving and struggle, the creation, in the form of evolved human beings, learn and acquire awareness of themselves and their environment. The rise in awareness of each individual, may in some way, enhance the awareness of the Creator Itself; how? and why? cannot be said with conviction, because of the inadequacy of facts available to man at the present time. This is also because it is not possible for the 'part' (man) to know the 'whole' (God). For further elaboration of this thought refer to the essay, 'The nature of a Natural Deity'. Just as a good teacher and an intelligent pupil join hands to advance knowledge and increase the level of total awareness around, so would both the Creator and the created affect each other on the subject of deciphering of the mysteries of the *Cosmic Consciousness*. This growth of consciousness of 'life' is really the manifesting of awareness for the Creator Itself, of It's own hidden and unfathomed, though, limitless abilities. What this means in simple terms is that with each new discovery man is gaining awareness of the hitherto unknown or unconscious phenomena which have always existed in the system, but have, so far, not been fathomed and understood by man. Having made the discovery, man now approaches the 'Creator-created' relationship with a bit of extra enlightenment.

Thus the entire phenomenon of creation by the Creator can be meaningful only if It (the Creator) acquires some satisfaction and Self-fulfillment from it. As seen in ' The nature of a Natural Deity', the Creator's own quest for conscious knowledge and awareness of Its reason for the creation is the only meaningful answer to the whole exercise of bringing it about. In this regard the accumulation of knowledge gained by the pupil and his intelligent contribution to it seems to evolve the entire 'System of creation' towards the fulfillment of its own purpose.

Chapter Nine

PHILOSOPHIC THOUGHT— SECULAR AND RELIGIOUS

It seems that most Philosophic ideas originated either in pre-renaissance Greece or post renaissance Europe. This is so because the majority of work done on the development of Philosophic thought has been undertaken by writers of the west, and perhaps for the western mind. Many Muslim and other thinkers and scholars of the intermediary period have been greatly acknowledged for their work in preserving the Greek and other ancient ideas, and then passing them on to the West. There, however, appears to be no clearly acknowledged influence of Islamic philosophy itself on the development of these thoughts. Conversely there also seems that outside philosophies have nothing to do in the evolution of Islamic thought itself. The impression that Islam developed in the isolation of the Arabian desert also seems to be a rather rudimentary approach. History shows that prophet Muhammad was quite well travelled before his ascendance to prophet-hood, and this surely exposed him to various rampant philosophies and ideas. His message shows a much wider connotation than the two previous Abrahamic religions of the region. An unbiased study of the religion of Islam points to the fact that it is perhaps an evolution of ideas of both Judaism and Christianity in consonance with a much wider world view. Any knowledge has a tendency to be influenced by ideas it is exposed to or gathers on its way through the times. So it seems rather unnatural that having passed through the hands of Muslim scholars the ideas would have filtered through their intellect and not picked up a tinge of the flavour of some their own thought. Retracing the path of progress in this field of human intellect reveals that a new and interesting phenomenon may have taken place during the bridging period, which for the Muslim's was the peak of their culture and civilization.

Now, the inhumane wars and wanton destruction during any period of history do not show much care for scholarship or intellectual achievement. A number of libraries and seats of learning were pillaged, burnt down and destroyed, surely wiping out and creating a gap and shortage of invaluable documents and scholarly material. Yet again, the Muslim civilization of Europe began its downward journey soon after the Crusades. This descent was two pronged. Internally, the suffocation took hold with the rise of totalitarianism and dogmatism, closing the gates of *Ijtehad* -- the questioning and redefining of established and outmoded ideas. On the external front was the fact that the most enlightened and developed part of the Islamic civilization bore the brunt of the Crusades and consequently suffered in their impetus of being the torch-bearers of learning and intellectual advancement.

The Muslim scholars have been rightly credited for their task of gathering, preserving and translating the work of Greek Philosophers. But for them, the dark ages would have engulfed all that had been achieved by previous intellectual enlightenment. Who can be accredited for doing a similar service for the preservation of the Muslim content in their contribution towards knowledge and its evolution ? None perhaps. Whatever has come to be handed down to the civilized society is the outcome of the remnants and leftovers of the plunderers and looters, and the remains of a rather prejudiced and perhaps misinformed enemy. The peacetime interaction between civilizations is a cultural exchange resulting in mutual growth of societies. Warring nations, on the other hand, have different priorities. The call to battle and its blind destruction are more immediate pursuits then. This is, perhaps, one reason for the ignorance about the Islamic ingredient in the realm of human thought, and natural prejudices may have added to the neglect. The thoughts of Renaissance and subsequent Philosophers are pregnant with feelings and sentiments for the Greek intellect, and seem to have taken up from where they left off. There is certainly a visible void or discontinuity in the otherwise continuous spectrum of human thought; Or, is it perhaps deliberate omission by some underlying, apparently subtle, yet deep rooted emotions ?

The prejudices are not imaginary but real, and had been fanned and inflated to play a role in discriminating against Muslim contribution to human civilization and the progress and development of human scholarship. Not only is this short sighted and unreal but limits the role of a parallel culture to mere translation and preservation of the past, which does not seem to fit in the natural scheme of change and evolution. It becomes rather evident if the history of the period is researched and traced from the starting of (say) the martyr movement in Spain in the ninth century.

The deep seated dislike for the phenomenal rise of the Islamic civilization can be seen from the historical background so eloquently narrated by 'Karen Armstrong' in 'Muhammad' (Chapter 1-- Muhammad the enemy). Some notable passages are.

"At that time Islam was a great world power while Europe, overrun by barbarian tribes, had become a cultural backwater. Later the whole world would seem to be Islamic, rather as it seems Western today, and Islam was a continuous challenge to the West until the

eighteenth century.

The loss of cultural roots can be a profoundly disturbing experience and even in our own day it can produce an aggressive, defiant religiosity as a means of asserting the beleaguered self. Perhaps we should remember the martyrs of Cordova when we feel bewildered by the hostility and rage in some of the Muslim communities in the West and in other parts of the world where Western culture threatens traditional values."

The strength and influence of Muslim culture had drawn the 'Mozarabs or *Arabisers'* – Christians who were admirers and supporters of Spain's Islamic culture – to take up the learning of this civilization's teachings, which seemed light years ahead of the rest of Europe.

Karen Armstrong continues:-

"The Christians love to read the poems and romances of the Arabs; they study the Arab theologians and philosophers, not to refute them but to form a correct and elegant Arabic. Where is the layman who now reads the Latin commentaries on the Holy Scriptures, or who studies the Gospels, prophets or apostles? Alas! All talented young Christians read and study with enthusiasm the Arab books."

Paul Alvaro, the Spanish layman who wrote this attack on the Mozarabs, at about the time of the Spanish martyr movement started after the incident of the monk Perfectus in the ninth century, saw Perfectus as a cultural and religious hero. Perfectus's denunciation of Muhammad had inspired a strange minority movement in Cordova whereby men and women presented themselves before the Qadi, the Islamic judge, and proved their Christian loyalty by a vitriolic and suicidal attack on the Prophet.

The martyr movement led by Alvaro and Eulogio was as bitterly opposed to the Christian Mozarabs as to the Muslims and accused them of being cultural defectors. Eulogio and Alvaro both believed that the rise of Islam was a preparation for the advent of Antichrist, the great pretender described in the New Testament, whose reign would herald the Last Days. The author of the second Epistle (letter)—St Paul in CA 51—to the newly founded church in Salonika, Greece, had explained that Jesus would not return until the 'great Apostasy' had taken place: a rebel would establish his rule in the temple of Jerusalem and mislead many Christians with his plausible doctrines. The Book of Revelations also spoke of a great Beast, marked with the mysterious number 666, who would crawl out of the abyss, enthrone himself on the Temple Mount and rule the world. Islam seemed to fit these ancient prophecies perfectly. The Muslims had conquered Jerusalem in 638, had built two splendid mosques on the Temple Mount and did indeed seem to rule the world. Even though Muhammad had lived after Christ, when there was no need for a further revelation, he had set himself up as a prophet and many Christians had apostatised and joined the new religion. Eulogio and Alvaro had in their possession a brief life of Muhammad, which had taught them that he had died in the Year 666 of the Era of Spain, which was thirty-eight years ahead of conventional reckoning. This late eighth century Western biography of Muhammad had been produced in the monastery of

Leyre near Pamplona on the hinterland of the Christian world, which trembled before the mighty Islamic giant. Besides the political threat, the success of Islam raised a disturbing theological question: how had God allowed this impious faith to prosper? Could it be he had deserted his own people? "

Observe the setting of the world stage at the time. As said earlier Muslim Spain was the seat of culture and learning, and Islamic civilization was at its peak. Europe, on the other hand, had been conquered by the barbarous tribes of Chengez and Halooku Khan. The glories of the Greek and Roman Civilizations had not only been brought to their knees, but were near annihilation had it not been preserved by the men of letters of Spain. The destruction of Europe is associated to the push of the Goths by the Huns and that they were nearly stampeded by these barbarians. There was not much left except fear and struggle for the very survival of the civilized human race.

The Crusaders also left an indelible mark of repugnant rejection of the values of the adversary. This is a natural consequence of enmity. The hate and dislike of each other took disproportionate heights by their ruthless massacre of both the Jews and the Muslims. That this is imbedded in the psyche of the following generations is evident from the literature generated in Europe during that period e.g. in the writings of Dante – Divine Comedy, Convivio, Monarchia etc.

The novelty and uniqueness of the Islamic philosophy is seen in its stress on the development of *'self-- governance of the free will'* and the *'implementation of the element of self --restraint'*. The self-governance and motivation of the free will and its conscious self-restraint are visible from the Qur'an's stress on personal uplift, and a constant evaluation of an individual's acts through a process of self-analysis ingrained in its tenets and teachings, and made achievable through the essence of its rituals.

The attempt here is to pick out some examples from thoughts of the renaissance and post- renaissance philosophers, thinkers and reformers and, look at them for influences of religious ingrain and subconscious effects of theological ideas. Monotheistic religions may have had the greatest influence on the psyche of these thinkers, and Islam being the most recent and evolved of the three, has been made a rational basis for the exercise.

SOME IDEAS OF THE PRE-RENNAISSANCE THINKERS

Plato

'The founder of Idealistic school of thought considered the world we see, touch, and experience through our senses as not real, nor a perfect world and is always changing. It is the impression of the ideas of some other idealistic world, which is perfect. He called this the world of "ideas". There is another principle in the Universe, that of 'matter'. This is all that ideas are not. It may be thought as the raw material upon which "ideas" or "forms" are impressed'.

Aristotle

'According to Aristotle 'forms' and 'ideas' are not outside matter. The 'forms' don't change but matter can. The acorn—in form is the same—but matter can change from acorn to tree to furniture; acquiring a different form as it changes. Matter changes and seeks to realise different forms—an acorn seeks to realise the form of an oak tree. A seed seeks to realise the form of a rose—Matter is thus, taking on, striving to realise forms.

For Aristotle all motion is to be explained as the union of form and matter. When matter offers resistance to form we have deformities, mistakes, evils. However matter is also a help to form in that it seeks to realise form, to become something….. There is a striving in the universe a seeking to become. Also the world is 'teleological' i.e. not a world of mere chance but one of purpose.

Thus, at one extreme we may think of pure matter without any form, formless matter. At the other extreme we may think of pure form, matterless form. But we cannot experience either. The things we experience in the universe is a world in which matter and form are united. And each object is the realisation of a form and is the matter for the realisation of still another form'.

EARLY CHRISTIAN THOUGHT

Apologists -- thinkers who sought to reconcile Christianity with Greek philosophy -- taught that the universe contains traces of something different from pure matter, and this points to God who is eternal, unchanging and good. For them, the 'ideas' of Plato and the 'forms' of Aristotle become God. <u>Everything in the world, in so far as it is a part of God, strives to be more like God, to return to Him</u>. (*See the similarity with the Quranic philosophy. (2: 156).*

Saint Augustine, who lived in the fourth century, taught that God created matter out of nothing. God created time and space also. Thus everything that is or ever shall be is a creation of God and must follow His laws and will.

Augustine came at a time that saw the degradation of the west. This lasted from about the fourth to the ninth century -- five hundred years. The period is remarkable for its meagreness of original thought and is thus termed the ' Dark Ages'. The one thing that flourished was the control of the institution of the Church. By the middle of the ninth century things started to improve. But by this time the Christian church was in complete control of Western Europe. It dominated everything, -- the state, education, peoples lives and thoughts. Thus all thinking was limited to church doctrines. *(See the present state of Muslim Umma).*

THE RENNAISSANCE AND POST-RENNAISSANCE THOUGHT

Unamuno

"The basic urge", thought Unamuno – Miguel De Unamuno, a Spanish poet, scholar and philosopher (1864 – 1936) – "--- is not simply to go on living, but to grow and develop." *(Does this not resonate the message of the Qur'an?)* " Therefore the fundamental problem of life is the necessity of coping with the idea of death, which stops all growth. Each man lives in the agony of conflict between his will's need for a life after death, and his reason's denial of life after death. If one is to exist in meaningful terms, one must accept this frustration, and in spite of the awareness of death one must will passionate action."

It is Nature's plan to incite man to action by inbreeding in him constant desire, want and need. Now, the continuity in the action of man is stopped by the same Nature, with the incorporation of death in his system. This is an apparent contradiction in Nature itself – only 'apparent'. The most convincing and a somewhat satisfying way to deal with this conflict is to see death differently. For, death may annihilate action but does not necessarily eradicate its effects or does away with all that has been done in life. It only truncates the material process of living, carrying forward the result of action in some other form, into the next phase of existence, and somehow also leaving a trace for posterity. It should therefore, not be considered that death ends existence altogether -- for living is a continuous process like so many other processes in nature. Only its form and manifestation may change upon physical death.

Now, that all natural phenomena are somehow continuous or inter connected is supported by Nature's laws of conservation. Take the example of the old scientific 'law of conservation of matter', which says – Matter can neither be created nor destroyed, what disappears in one form reappears in some other. This law was, however, amended after its renunciation by the theory of relativity, which now incorporates the inter-changeability of matter and energy. In either case the continuity of natural phenomena is maintained. Let's take another example from science. Electromagnetic radiations exist in a continuous range of frequencies. Starting from the ultra-violet range through to the infra-red. Only a small portion of this continuous range of vibrations is normally discernible, and is called the visible spectrum. The frequencies of vibrations extend unendingly both in the infra- red and the ultra- violet regions, and continue in both directions of the spectrum of visible light. Yet again, matter exists in an array of sizes. Starting from sub-atomic particles to supra-celestial bodies. Only a small range of sizes can be seen by an unaided eye. To study others a microscope, telescope or other instruments are required. The whole array of creation thus seems to be continuous. Clearly then we should not doubt the continuity of the phenomena of existence, only a portion of which is discernible - - from the cradle to the grave -- that is what we commonly call life.

Hegel

"George William Friedrich Hegel 1770 – 1831, the famous German philosopher, <u>held that the Universe is a process of evolution in which that which was inherent at the beginning is finally realised</u>." *(This again is an Islamic concept, where it has been expanded to say that 'man is made of the finest ingredients' and is capable of realising the inherent goal –Al Qur'an*

95: 4to 6) "In this realisation the part seeks to become itself the Full. The rose, for example, is inherent in the seed, and is the result of the process of evolution from seed to rose. However, the seed is not fully itself until the rose has bloomed. This is true of the Universe, Hegel believed. Since God is, for Hegel, the living, moving reason of the world, *He becomes fully conscious and the Universe becomes fully realised only in the minds of human beings. The self conscious individual is the fullest realisation of the Universe.....*" (This concept has been furthered and elaborated in the essay 'The nature of a Natural Deity')

" Progress for Hegel, is the development of the consciousness of freedom....."

" Man is free, but he is free to realise the nature of the Universe. In realising this nature, he is realising himself. Therefore, man is free to realise himself to the fullest..."

The overtones of Hegel's thought are themselves an evolution from the Greek, through the Arabs, to his own age. Read closely the above clearly shows that religious philosophy is evident and predominant in human thought. Now whether Judaism and / Or Christianity are as explicit in their theories of evolution as Hegel is, cannot be said; but that this is the Quran's central theme can be authenticated from its various verses. -- ' **Indeed your returning is to Us'** -- or the likes of it, are continuously emphasised in it. Now the return to the source by man is the completion of his being. *Seen in a slightly broader context, it becomes the realisation for both man and God, because both are equally dependent on the other for their individual fulfillment.* This idea is discussed in more detail in the essay, ' The nature of a Natural Deity'. *It is felt that in the example of the rose and the seed, one aspect seems to have been overlooked. The rose is inherent in the seed and the seed fulfills itself upon its bloom. The cycle does not stop here. It is continuous as the rose carries* *the ingredient of its own perpetuation, by containing in itself a new seed for pollination and regeneration. This leads us to another aspect of the process, the cyclic or immortal behaviour of Nature. Or seen differently, the genius of Nature's plan by being the inherent necessity of the whole process itself. (This concept is visible in the Quran, 112:2. Translated as, 'God the immanently indispensable'). Seen in this light it is gathered that one cannot fulfill its purpose without the other i.e. God cannot achieve fulfillment without humans and vice versa.* This interconnection of the human and the Deity are the extrapolation of Hegel's philosophy seen through the teachings of religion. Or in a more philosophic terminology, that the man , 'matter' -- seeks to attain the 'Form' -- God. Matter itself could have come from an 'Idea' or 'Form', and going through various cycles of change or 'realizations' – in other words evolution – is seeking to return to the original state of origination.

The question is Why and what does it hope to accomplish in the process? (Refer to 'The nature of a Natural Deity'.)

In the unfolding of the process the *System* has a tendency to gather information or awareness of *Itself* as it goes along. The whole process starts from the premise of dormant 'unconscious consciousness' through a peak of 'conscious consciousness' and returns to a stable state of 'conscious unconsciousness'. To elaborate this statement let us take the example of human beings. A child begins to explore the world and his environment through a means of trial and error. He/ she observes, experiments and starts becoming aware and conscious of things. Having acquired knowledge of a set of things, he/ she is said to have become conscious or aware of them. The attention is then turned to a new set of things and ideas, and so the level of awareness keeps evolving. Storing the information and processing it by the help of the intellect and the mind results in the increase of knowledge. This is the stage when the child is becoming 'unconsciously conscious'. Having reached the prime of life his / her confidence has reached its peak and all faculties are at an optimum level. This is the stage when one is 'consciously conscious' -- In full control of the situation to the best of one's abilities. Now, when the aging process sets in, a person begins to accept the finiteness of things and true reality begins to dawn, and one is at the beginning of the phase of 'consciously unconsciousness'. The above example is a general over view. Exceptions are always there.

Whether it was Islam that developed from the Greeko-Christian philosophy or it was the renaissance philosophers who adopted Islamic ideas cannot be said. However, taking into consideration the continuity and evolution of knowledge, some effect of each must have been carried forward by the passage of time. Considering the conditions of the time and the limitations of communications it is quite possible that various novel ideas may have all been original in themselves, and may have dawned in complete isolation and quarantine from each other, in different parts of the globe. The level of human grasp and comprehension seem to be uniform and people everywhere, be it East or West, tackle similar problems and solve similar mysteries, in similar ages of time. That this is so is due to the fact that the awareness level of humanity increases with each new discovery or finding by man in any part of the world. Also perhaps the development and evolution of the world keeps in step all through time and age. If this can be proven then it goes to show that awareness level of all humanity increases uniformly, though at any individual level each has a personal level of growth, but at the cumulative level the whole world progresses by the discovery of a new phenomenon. In order to tackle this question one has to study the level of human endeavour at different periods of human history. By the level of endeavour is meant the total capability of humanity in a given age of civilization. To begin with, human society was nomadic and lived by gathering and hunting; then came the agrarian period to be followed by the development of trade and cottage industry. The greatest revolution in the level of human endeavour and achievement came with the industrial age. In the beginning an individual's achievement took a longer time to show affect to the world, but today with modern means of communication a single idea has the capability of influencing the entire globe instantaneously. This gives man the power to bring about change with tremendous speed. We have gained both speed and knowledge to change the world as a whole. It remains to be seen which direction mankind will take with these powerful tools now available at their disposal. They can fight evil and conquer it or become its victims and be conquered.

Sufism And Islam

Only change is permanent. For any idea to acquire a perpetual mode it must either accept change, or itself influence and bring about change. Islam is such an idea, because it is based on Natural axioms which stand the test of time and age, and that change itself comes about on the basis of these axiomatic truths.

The contention, by one school of thought, that Sufism is not Islam, is a very categorical statement. Its truth will depend on one's perception of Islam and Sufism. In this world there is very little distinct black and white, and a lot of grey. There is also very little of independence and a lot more of interconnection and dependence between various things and phenomena.

The article "Sufism: Its Origins" (courtesy Al-Haramain Foundation) gives a historical account of the development of the philosophy. It is said there that:

" Although it (Sufism) began as a move towards excessive *Ibaadah* (worship), such practices were doomed to lead to corruption, since their basis did not come from authentic religious doctrines, but rather exaggerated human emotions. Sufism as an organized movement arose among pious Muslims as a reaction against the worldliness of the early Umayyad period (AD 661 – 750)".

It is clear here that the practice of the puritanical teachings of Islam were either too rigid, or on the other hand were being overshadowed by the glamour of materialism, emanating from the freedom of the will over the dictates of the orthodoxy. In any case a reactionary movement set in, in the form of Sufism. The advent of the movement should be seen as an outcome of the effect of changes in the practice of Muslims. The present material race on the one hand and the antagonistic fundamental orthodoxy on the other, seem to present an identical situation and an ideal time for the revival of some similar movement, this time in the world at large. This idea is supported and confirmed by the recent 'hippie' culture of the last century. A rise of such a rejectionist tendency in humans is seen as a natural balancing act born out of the extreme swings of the pendulum of their conflicting ideologies. It is pertinent to quote Philip K Hitti from his book, 'History of the Arabs', and what he says about the closing of the Pre-Islamic age: ' The stage was set, the moment was psychological, for the rise of a great religious and national leader '. Now perhaps for the rise of a new world order, having universal acclaim and adaptability, an 'Ideology' based on the dictates of Nature, encompassing the laws of ' Cause and Effect', may provide the answer. Islam, if seen in the correct perspective and understood in a rational manner, has the ingredients of a self-correcting and self- perpetuating dynamic social order based on the axioms of Nature. Its message and philosophy if correctly fathomed has all the ingredients of a lasting Universal order. One such Universal idea for the present concerted and collaborative world development is the onset of a rational and conscious surrender of the surplus each individual possesses or acquires. The redistribution and reallocation of national wealth and eventually the worldly wealth is the need of the hour. The movement of the 99% v/s the 1% of the present time is the beginning of the calling for the conscious realization of the demand for survival of the human race itself.

If we humans do not see the light of the day in time before the sun sets, it will none the less set at its appointed time, leaving none but us in the darkness to perish due to our own misdeeds. The earth will continue to turn and the planets will continue to orbit the sun, only the earthlings will have been annihilated as per their own wrong doings and the fulfillment of the predictions of the theory of 'Gaia'.

Chapter Ten
RELIGIOUS MYTHS AND REALITY

The recent surfacing of the ancient manuscript of the gospel of Judas has wide ranging repercussions, these are being presently debated anew. It is interesting to note that a lot of interest has also been generated by the court case on Dan Brown's novel ' The Da Vinci Code', where it is claimed by Michael Baigent, Leigh and Lincoln, the authors of ' Holy blood, Holy grail', that Dan Brown infringed the idea of his novel from their book. The other relevant sources of interest in this new trend of research on Christianity would be ' The Gospel according to Jesus Christ' by Jose Saramago, 'Mary called Magdalene' by Margaret George, 'The Jesus Papers' by Michael Baigent, and of special mention is Reza Aslan's Zealot.

The religion of Islam too is also presently being scrutinized and debated at various levels and in diverse forums, primarily since the episode of 9/11. Both outsiders and the Muslims themselves are ill at ease with the present status of many religious interpretations of Islam and the ever-strong hegemony of the Mullah. The orthodox and dogmatic clergy of Islam hold the religion hostage, much like the Papacy does of Christianity. The one, in the case of Islam, draw their strength from the Book, ' The Qur'an', which is the center of Islam's adherence. The other, in the case of Christianity, draw their power from the Church which created the center – ' The Bible' – from the sayings of Christ as collected and composed by his disciples. The propagators of both faiths zealously guard the basis of their beliefs in their respective Books.

All, so called heavenly revealed books, are based on the 'common axioms of Nature', and the laws of 'cause and effect'. They aim to uplift the morality of human beings beyond their animal instincts and help in their evolution to higher stations in life. Each successive message of the Torah, Bible and the Qur'an are themselves an evolution, one over the other. This is indicative of the readjustment of the human thought itself with the passage of time, and increase in knowledge and awareness. Whereas it is seen that the Torah is mainly based on oral tradition, which was the order of the day, the Bible is a relatively more advanced collection of ideas and thoughts of Christ, through the written gospels of his disciples. The Qur'an is supposedly a verbatim recording of the utterances of Prophet Muhammad. Whatever be the means and method of the gathering of various religious ideas and their message, it is quite evident that a progression, in both their method and content, is the outcome of an evolved state of the art of communication, both between human beings themselves and also the Deity, the Creator or the Source.

This recent revival of curiosity in the religious field is bound to have repercussions not only for Christianity but other monotheistic faiths as well. All of whom have one thing in common, that of projecting the Creator as exhibiting basic human traits, both in feelings and emotions. In other words they have created an anthropomorphic Deity in order to project It, and understand It in human terms. This came about with man's need and desire to comprehend the whole phenomenon of creation, and to make some sense out of it. This anthropomorphic concept however, has its limitations, in as much as humans have their own. In some religions and philosophies like Buddhism, Zen and even mystic traditions of monotheism itself, the Deity does not seem so human. A rather abstract and a metaphysical Being, recognized more by the pervading spirit than by Its mere human like traits. The road to the Ultimate is through a more self-lifting and a rather elevating spiritual approach; a sort of blending between the mind, body and soul—the triad of human existence. They try to reach the Source, if you like upwards, rather than bringing It down to their own level, as seen in the anthropomorphic approach. The other disadvantage of orthodox anthropomorphism is that a via media -- a priest or a saint like personality is needed to forward the dictates or messages of the Deity. In classic monotheistic doctrines there is also a compulsion to unify and gather together, to amalgamate, in a way to shrink, rather than develop and diversify individuality. This, either knowingly or inadvertently leads to imitating, following, and personality worship as against getting to the essence of the message and implementing its teachings as per individual requirement and acceptability. Monotheistic religions are mainly geared towards regimentation and uniformity of practice rather than freedom of adaptation of the essence of the message as suits the individual's need or requirement. It is like an army camp where the training starts with early morning rise, drill and parade. Then specific meals, at specific times are served in a regimental environment, usually with a fixed menu and controlled quantity. All this is geared to a purpose of complete submission to the will of the superiors and a blind following of their orders. Perhaps this is essential to create an environment to get concerted, unquestioning and unidirectional effort. Real life, however, is different, where each person lives as an individual and leads a separate life, faced with unique and different problems, and each one having different potentialities and priorities. Each one's nature and reaction is different and so also the extent of one's feelings. The basic general need of people may be similar, e.g. the need for food, shelter and clothing. The achievement of which may, however, be done by different methods and means, and also of different quality and quantity.

The main purpose of religious pursuit is to groom and uplift each individual to perform some acts for a common benefit, and some others to raise one's self to the extent of one's full capacity. Man has thus to learn both to cooperate for the common good of mankind and yet compete for excellence at the individual level.

The basis of the Christian church is being quite openly questioned, and it seems to stand on shaky ground ever since 'The Da Vinci Code' raised various queries about Jesus and his lineage. Add to this the question about Christ's divinity, which has been quite vociferously raised in 'Jesus Papers' and other such publications. The impact and influence of religion on human life seems to have lessened with the advancement of knowledge and the increase of information with the advancement in technology. This is perhaps so because the fear of the unknown has receded and the material glitter of the present life has made the 'here' and 'now' more interesting than the future and its uncertainties. Globalization too is playing its own role in the evolution of human thought. Seeing this trend of probe, and the acceleration of interest in religion in general, and Islam in particular since 9/11, has made people turn to look at it more closely. Slowly but surely, both from within and without the belief system itself, voices are being raised for its critical analysis and more openness in its study. This has prompted thoughts of a reformation in the whole idea of religion and religious beliefs.

The two main sources of Islam are 'The Qur'an' (The book) and 'Sunnah' (The practices of Prophet Muhammad). While the Qur'an is considered the word of God and is said to have come and been compiled in the full light of history, Muslims are in a complete awe and reverence of it and refuse to consider changing its single word. The doings and the sayings of the Prophet, however, have been noted and recorded by his followers, much like that in the case of Jesus Christ. Whereas it is undesirable to tamper with the message and its recording, it is relatively easy to question the method and content of the 'Hadees' (The supposed sayings and doings of Prophet Muhammad), the bulk of which were recorded well after the Prophet's death.

That, the Prophets, Sages, Sufis, Mystics and other similar beings are men of exceptional spiritual and mental capabilities should not be doubted. They are certainly people who may have reached a different dimension even in this earthly life. They are seen to have a keen and sharp foresight, and are able to fathom phenomenon everyone cannot—Phenomena of the mind, body and the soul. They are surely more evolved in their personalities than ordinary human beings. Nonetheless they are from the same human race, and must exhibit and conform to basic human traits and requirements of the body to sustain them in the first place. Only their understanding and control of it is more profound and comprehensive as compared to others.

A genius is one who can think and comprehend beyond the ordinary and then also act above the ordinary level to implement his ideas. Thinking and fathoming is the function of the mind, but action and implementation is the function of the body. When both are above the norm the individual evolves to the next level of existence, and reaches other dimensions. There is, however, a fine dividing line between genius and madness. When knowledge and awareness is consciously achieved and knowingly harmonized with action one remains in the domain of sanity. If the marriage of the two is uncontrolled and incoherent it leads to the realm of imbalance. A genius's ever lasting quality is his depth of knowledge and awareness. The result is a vast variety of shades of impressions; taking into consideration new slants and possibilities, hence the acceptance and admiration of facts and ideas beyond common comprehension.

All original thinkers have sensitivity about them. They are aware and gain consciousness of phenomena which are beyond ordinary humans and want to share it with the world; only to be resisted and ridiculed by conformists and propagators of status quo, who do not want the existing order of things to be changed or modified. Original thought leads to the reality of extreme loneliness and elevated comprehension, and is insatiable by temporary companionships one finds in the surroundings. Keeping a balance within the constitution of the 'Self' and the 'Over-self' is the most difficult task. This can only be done with the inculcation of discipline and justice in thought, word and deed, at all times.

A state of serenity or bliss is sought by man since the beginning of time. It may not be achievable in this mortal life but its search is eternal and has been endowed in human nature. Self fulfillment is one form of acquiring it. Contentment comes in spurts and bliss and satisfaction are temporarily achieved when man puts in his best and whole-hearted effort in exposing the hidden embedded talent, possessed by every individual; thus fulfilling the very purpose of his creation perhaps. The liberation of the trapped treasures of one's nature is every ones desire, but the majority of us are lost and tangled in the achievement of glamour and material glitter of this worldly life. Only some can see the truth beyond its physical garb. The prophets and the like saw it and wanted to spread it around.

The one distinctive aspect between man and the rest of the creation is his intellect. As all things have good or bad effects depending on how they are viewed and employed, so also it is with the intellect. If intellect is endowed with a positive approach it leads to progress and achievement, but if enshrined in pessimism it destroys and destructs the edifice of life itself. The basis of intellect is thought and imagination. Out of which emerge all word and deed. A beautiful thought emanates from purity and good intent, and a vicious idea takes birth in the ugliness of contamination. Purity in its turn is fostered by faith and belief, whereas impurity originates in doubt and deceit.

With this background in mind if we reflect on the person and nature of Prophets, Sages, Sufis and others, we conclude that all of them are looking for 'Truth' in their own way. It is only natural that having found it they want to share it and impart it to others. That these souls are at different levels of comprehension and mental activity is evident from each one's message. Having achieved or reached these levels, either they are differently made, or have acquired them after intense and rigorous self-discipline and training, makes them unique and different from the common man. Whatever be the case, they attain a communication with the 'Source' -- call it one's Inner- self, Over-self, Spirit, God, or what you will. This Other-self is surely connected with the Self in some way or the other. The exact means and method of It's contact and communication has yet to be fully understood. The greatest understanding of this phenomenon, so far, has come about in the fields of Psychology and Philosophy. They may not be able to fully explain all its aspects, but are none the less, engaged in trying to understand it at rational levels.

Humans are a 'holonistic' development of animals; meaning, that they are an evolution over the animal structure in nature, having transcended and further evolved in certain traits. Their main area of evolution is in the mental process, i.e. they have developed mentally over other preceding species in Nature's scheme of things, and also their own previous generations. This is a logical conclusion taking into consideration that the knowledge or the information content of the world is increasing with the passage of time, and this increased content of information is bound to lead to a new world, much different from its past. where it was certainly in a more ignorant condition. In order to keep pace with change human capabilities would also have to increase, expand or evolve. Now, mind and intellect are the areas where further development is likely and possible for man to progress, as at the level of the body no change has been observed over the centuries, and there, evolution seems to have peaked. Humans will however, continue to exhibit all traits of his animal ancestry e.g. the requirement of food, sexual multiplication and need to preserve the environment if he is to continue to remain alive. A neglect of any of these will reverse the evolutionary cycle, and then instead of progress decay will set in.

The next step in the journey of human evolution seems to be a development of a more logical approach in all fields of knowledge, religion being no exception. Religious myth will be replaced with rational and logical ideas and the basic axioms of humanity will become the basis of 'humanism'. This new trend of humanism has all the ingredients of religious thought. It however, manifests a practical and practicable aspect of all faiths. Humanism, consciously or unconsciously, in actuality is really the practical implementation of religious ideals. To verify this let us examine some deep rooted myths of religion and see if they can stand the test of logic and common sense. And, if they cannot then they will either be discarded, or will by themselves wither away with the passage of time.

Many phenomena described in various religious literatures seem rather irrational and farfetched. They may have been plausible to be accepted by the level of mind of that period. As said earlier, evolution seems to be Nature's way of change towards development, or degradation. Evolution in all aspects of the human triad, of thought, word or deed is the method adopted by Nature to transform the human race and even the rest of the creation, the rate of change however, may be different for different things. Now, change is the only permanent component in nature, stagnation in life is death for the living. This means that while inanimate objects may retain their construction and structures for a longer period of time, they too modify and change, and play a part in the process of evolution of life in some form or the other. For, it is through the exchange, readjustment or transfer of these materials that the living things survive and thrive. If the process of evolution is helpful in the growth of life, progress is made, otherwise the outcome is annihilation. If the above is concurred with, then human beings must have evolved over the years and will continue to do so. Now, for human evolution to take effect the triad of thought, word and deed would alter with the passage of time. New ideas would take birth and with them new acts and deeds. Let us look at some examples of these religious myths and see how they may correspond with reality.

Noah, one of the earliest prophets of monotheism, is said to have gathered a pair of each species of animals and his own family, and sailed in the Arc to avoid the deluge. In the mythical floods that followed all those left behind perished and the world seems to have started anew from those that took the boat. Creation, it seems had developed incorrigible sins and ills and Nature or God had to do what He did, and then started with a clean slate. This whole story raises the first and basic question about God's omniscience. How can a Deity which is supposed to be such, had no knowledge that His creation was going to do 'this' or 'that' in the future? That only after seeing the spread of sin and corruption He took the drastic action of exterminating all but a few, and to start all over again? On the other hand if God did not know that people would behave such then He cannot have been All Knowing. Whatever be the reason for God to have behaved as He did, Noah on the other hand, certainly acted

on human instinct of 'faith' and 'belief'. That having got the revelation or intuition he built the Arc and set sail trusting his God would not let him down. This shows that the myths may not be rationally convincing but the morals they present are exemplary and meaningful i.e. without faith and belief deep rooted change and progress is difficult to achieve.

The incident of Abraham's offering to sacrifice his son and the appearance of a sheep in its place cannot be taken to have occurred literally. If the thought process of Abraham is analyzed it is logical to conclude, that he being a devout and pious man, must have wanted to thank the Deity for having blessed him with the son in his old age. He must have thought deep and hard to come up with a worthy gift for his God. The most worthy and the dearest of his possessions was the gift he had himself received. Now to return the gift one has received is a rather rude way of saying ' thank you, but no thank you'. And, for his God to have put the demand for the sacrifice is also illogical, because God must have known well that if the son is actually sacrificed there would be no human way to fulfill His own promise to Abraham, that of making his seed multiply and be numerous. Once again the human, Abraham, is seen to have acted on his firm faith and belief that the God who had given him the son in his dotage would surely be able to give him others to fulfill His promise. So Abraham's readiness to sacrifice is plausible, because he would have believed in the supreme act of self-sacrifice to achieve self-amelioration, but God's demand of it is preposterous. Never the less it is once again the moral or the

lesson of the myth that has to be absorbed. For, if the mythical episode had been followed in letter, most male descendents would not have survived the knife of their fathers, and it seems doubtful if every human offering would have been replaced by a sheep. The moral or the lesson Abraham must have learnt from the episode is again of faith and belief in the promise of the deity, and that the road to self amelioration is to be ready for any sacrifice in the way of God. And the act of self sacrifice is the will power to control ones unbridled desires of wants and the avarice of material needs.

\# Moses is claimed to have parted the Red Sea to take his people across; but then as the forces of the Pharaoh followed the sea closed upon them and they drowned. The conviction and belief of a leader takes his nation to unknown destinations. The strength of his conviction is the motivating power but the might of the resolution of the populace is really the implementing force, because in numbers is strength which a single individual cannot exhibit. The leader may be instrumental in showing the way but it is the momentum generated by the people that push the idea forward. Once set in motion it only takes the leader's foresight and honest belief in the plan, and sensible guidance to reach it to the point of fruition. As said earlier, reward and success originate in the purity of intention, whereas deceit of revenge leads to a doubtful conclusion. So, whether it was low tide at the time of Moses' crossing, and that the tide had changed when Pharaoh came along, or it was the sheer struggle for survival of the Jews, who were fighting for their life, that got most of them across, and the doubt deceit in the enemy that kept him behind, cannot be ascertained. The moral of the story however is clearly the conclusion that faith and belief coupled with sacrifice and determination bring out the best in people in the most impossible of circumstances.

Jesus Christ is said to have had the power to raise the dead. Whether the raising of the dead means the bringing into life of a physically dead person, or it signifies the infusion of life in the down trodden and humiliated people to be able to get up and struggle to turn the tide, is the debate. Seeing the state of the Jews and the distortion of the purity of their religion must have influenced and moved Jesus to preach and project his new and radical teachings. By steadfastly staying on the path of his resolve, so much so that he went to the gallows instead of giving in, showed the followers that in death is true meaning of life. Jesus' crucifixion kept his message alive. For, had he died any other way, he may not have left behind such a powerful lesson to wake the people out of their slumber and dope, and virtually rise them from the dead.

Prophet Muhammad is yet another example of the spiritually uplifted and refined human beings. Being extremely humble, very meditative and a deep thinker, he was unusually concerned about the sad state of affairs of humanity. It is said that while engrossed in meditation and devotion, in the cave, he was visited by an angel who revealed to him the message of the Qur'an. This is another example of the rise of the spiritual Self to the

extent where the two, the Over Self and the Self, are harmonized and fused, opening the mind and vision to extraordinary levels, resulting in the fathoming of uncommon phenomena and the acquisition of above normal faculties. The Prophet must have risen himself to such elevated spiritual dimensions that the Over Self could not be constrained to reveal Itself, imparting knowledge and awareness to the seeker. Revelation would really be the release of the deepest of human thought that lies buried in the personality of the deepest of thinkers. Only those few individuals who have raised themselves to the peak of self control and dedicated self sacrifice may become capable of seeing and uniquely understanding the working of the gist of Natural laws.

Now, whatever may be the reality of an angel and the message's mode of descent, one thing is certain that Prophet Muhammad's understanding and preaching of it was definitely the work of a genius. If his message is read objectively, it shows the Prophet's unparallel ability of both Self-attachment and Self-detachment with life and its true meaning. The first and the most important example of it is that the Prophet does not take any credit for the message's content and reveals it as God's word. This is remarkable, in as much as, even if it was not, the messenger is absolved of any wrongdoing or shortcomings in the message, as the oneness of it then rests on God. Further, this method of propagation got the message an undivided attention and remarkable reception. The Prophet was acclaimed as the only worthy recipient of it and he killed two birds with one stone; getting the message across and with as little as possible resistance to its unusual content, and the staging of revolutionary change in many deep rooted orthodox values of the society; Noteworthy, being the abolishing of idols, the problem of slavery, the raising status of women, disbursement of wealth etc. The dictates were unusual, because they were extraordinary for the time and situation, and also because they took root from the lessons of the two earlier systems of Judaism and Christianity. Islam evolved from them and took naturalism further than the other two had.

From the above it is evident that the spiritually uplifted humans were surely extraordinary people, who all had the good of humanity at heart. They were people of sheer goodwill and desired genuine uplift of humanity. They certainly believed in the extraordinary messages they were presenting to the simple and humble people around them, and to make it fathomable they had to rely on the mythology and methodology of the period. For, were they to speak in non-anthropomorphic terms, the concept of the Deity would never have been understood so clearly and would not have taken hold. One has to speak to the other person in his language to communicate and achieve one's motive better. If for nothing else then for these qualities alone, apart from any mythological overbearing, these stalwarts of humanity should be acknowledged and revered. Karen Armstrong, in her book ' A short history of myth' has very aptly phrased the use of myth and mythology when she says , " Correctly understood, the lessons of mythology puts us in the correct spiritual or psychological posture for right action, in this world or the next".

Chapter Eleven
FUNDAMENTALS OF FUNDAMENTALISM

To understand fundamentalism one has to look at its fundamental properties. Fundamentally, any living system, be it human or non-human, exhibits the most fundamental of requirements, and that is, ' an innate property to seek to preserve itself'. No sacrifice is great enough to make in order to continue to survive and hold on to dear life. Be it one's desire, need or duty, the preservation of every life is essential for the flourishing of humanity and civilization, so much so, that even dissent and opposition must be tolerated, even if for nothing else then its negative value alone.

Humans, who have in some way developed and evolved over the animal, continue to, and will, exhibit their basic animal traits along with some other form of a more developed behaviour, which they may have acquired on account of their intellect. This intellectual activity is a human's most distinguishing characteristic over other forms of life. Due to their capacity to think and consciously analyze, understand and manipulate the surroundings humans seek not only to live, but also to do so with a reason. The reason for existence is sought and held on to in a variety of ways – differing from people to people. Whichever method is most convincing and suits the individual becomes the basis of their justifying themselves and the world around, and this they tend do with a passionate conviction.

If religion seems convincing to some people, they try not only to live by it themselves but wish others to do so too. If scientific laws are the dependable vehicles for some other people, they examine things around them based on those principles and expect of others to do the same. If the laws of material economics give satisfactory explanation to yet some others, then they tend to explain every thing in material terms and want people to follow their train of thought. Thus, it is the mindset of individuals that makes them accept a set of ideas, and affords them the dependable reason to acquire a peace within and outside of themselves, and gives a meaning and reason to their lives.

The moment one's belief is shaken, either by questioning, or is found to be inadequate to explain certain phenomena, the common reaction is to defend it rather than accept change and adjust one's own thinking accordingly. This inertia to avoid change leads some people to re-examine the basis of their ideas and find solutions within the framework of the belief itself, and, then take it upon themselves, as if it were their duty, to enforce it ever more vehemently on everyone around. This is so because human nature is possessive, protective and projective of what it sees to be its precious belonging, and that which it does not want to give up easily.

Now, only some few things seem to be the real essentials for existence. Primarily they are: nourishment, preservation and reproduction. These are the requirements for every life on an individual and a collective basis. The first duty is to the self, and after having satisfied that need one looks towards the propagation of the group as a whole, for there is strength in numbers. Things like environment, natural resources and even ideas and beliefs are a collective possession, and are thus needed to be commonly shared and jointly guarded.

In the animal kingdom the basis of survival is seen to be the fitness to stand and tackle the existing situation and predominantly fend for the self, and Nature and its laws do the rest. For humans however, it is not sufficient to survive in the present alone but also to intelligently maneuver and plan for a future to their liking. Now, to be able to willfully gain in the times to come it is imperative to learn from the past and utilize those experiences in the present. But, somehow humans get so carried away by the desires of the future that they tend to forget the past, forego the present, and ignore the fact that evolution into the next phase will only be based on these two previous conditions of time.

If the situation shows a tendency to change, life tends to readjust to the circumstance. At the animal level this is seen to be brought about by an instinctive, unconscious mechanism of readjustment. Humans, however, should either be convinced of the necessity for change or must themselves understand and reason out its inevitability. Even then, the inertia mentioned above, is the factor that holds back the individual from recognizing the facts immediately. In fact the usual human response is to fight the change and try to alter the circumstance and the environment itself, in order to fit it into the scheme of their desires.

The logical extension of the consequence to preserve life is to then perpetuate and finally immortalize it. This is somehow achievable by passing the essence of ones own experiences on to the succeeding generations – for, otherwise why else would there be the need to reproduce and propagate? The birds and the bees do it as per the dictates of Nature. Humans follow it too, but being thinking animals they desire not only to perpetuate their physical selves but also their ideas and beliefs along with it. The fundamentality of the mentality which one tries to propagate and promote, from the past to the present and into the future is, however, bound by a redefining and modification at every successive step of the way; again by Nature under its laws of evolution. Consciously or not, the idea itself traverses a different set of circumstance on its journey from the past generation to the present before it is ready to leap into the future. It must readjust itself in order to smoothly interface with the evolving situation. For, otherwise, the existing idea will nonetheless have to submit and conform to the greater and superior forces of Nature, or otherwise be left behind and then eliminated. Inertia once again resists this transition and tends to maintain the status quo.

Having borne with the discourse so far we can now take the plunge into the topic of the day. A fundamental mindset is none else than this inertia in the thought process of the fundamentalist. It is ones innate desire to stay in the comfort zone and to maintain the status quo. The basic idea is the foundation on which one builds the edifice of society and so does not want to change it. As one tries to achieve immortality, one realizes that it can only be possible by passing on the basic principles, inherited or acquired, to the next generation. Also, one does not wish the progeny to repeat the mistakes one has committed in one's own life. The approach then is to forcefully or adamantly reinforce the foundation as firmly as possible into their minds.

Now, most things usually have two effects, a positive and a negative, a ying and a yang. What is positive or constructive in one situation may sometimes become negative or obstructive in another, as also, one man's meat may be another man's poison. Let us take an example to explain this. 'Friction' is a resistive force that restricts motion. On the other hand if there were no friction things would not stay in one place. e.g. a car would not stop if there was no friction between the earth and its tires. But the same friction has to be overcome and harnessed in order to set the car in motion. What an irony, that, what is essential in one situation is a hindrance in another. This is why friction has been called 'a necessary evil', and hence the corollary that ' evil too is a necessity'. This situation occurs at many stages in life. Fundamentalism also follows the same rule and shows two sides, it can be both devolutionary as well as evolutionary. It is both an extrovert and an introvert phenomenon. That it is extrovert is clearly exhibited by the behaviour of those trying to impose it on others. It's being introvert is far more subtle, invisible and deep rooted in the psyche. The holding on to dogma, by the fundamentalists, is due to their fear of the unknown, which in reality is that ' indeterminate part of one's own unconscious self' which resists being brought to the surface where it can be rationally handled. This again is due essentially to the pervading inertia. If the saying, ' the greatest thing to fear is fear itself', is accepted and believed, much dogmatism and orthodoxy would be overcome by a logical acceptance of reality. Fundamentalism may be essential to build a system but then it also becomes its adhesive force that resists change. Fundamentalism usually starts out as a defensive measure. One looks to protect the basis of ones beliefs and ideals. It, however, becomes retaliatory in outlook if the fear of one's own annihilation gets deep rooted, for then it acquires a mode of ' offence is the best defense', and that is what eventually makes it derogatory.

All stable systems in nature, be they ' macro-systems' e.g. the solar system or 'micro-systems' e.g. the classical atomic structure, are both balanced and evolving. It is seen that the achievement of balance, in the various forces in any natural system, is an evidence of the probability of its survival and progress. For, imbalance is usually only a temporary, floating phenomenon and must eventually reach some state of adjustment and stability for the survival of the system as a whole. Taking lesson from this it is imperative that humans too should learn to balance and evolve in their thought, word and deed for sensible survival, and progress of the species as a whole.

In the closing I leave with a hope that it will perhaps be noted that an attempt has been made to tackle the basis of the problem of fundamentalism from a slightly different angle and a fresh approach, and that the microscope has, however, been pointed towards the root cause of the situation.

I must admit that it is not essential that everyone would see eye to eye and agree with the ideas and the projections of this essay; and so I am tempted to quote Ghalib, the famous poet philosopher of the East, when he says:

> *Ya rub neh who sumjhay hain neh sumjhain gay mare baat*
> *Dai aur dil ous ko joh neh dai mujah ko zubaan aur.*

O Lord, they do not comprehend
Nor ever will acclaim.
Give to them a new heart,
If not me another tongue, to proclaim.

Chapter Twelve

A MUSLIM'S DESTINY

With so much of advancement in the world and so much of information explosion, it is perhaps pertinent to examine the basics of religious thought and look at the foundations and fundamentals of Islam from a new angle, without the help of the self entrenched experts and adamant promoters of status quo. Amongst the distorted fundamentalists there are bound to be some who ask themselves the reason for this violent conflict of ideologies when the axioms of all religious beliefs are similar. For, no religion teaches to steal or murder, destroy or plunder. In fact the pursuit of every religious thought is to build, to advance and to uplift human beings. So no religious ideology should promote the annihilation of morals of others for the sake of its own selfish propagation. Therefore let us, on our own, try and explore the basics without provoking the conflict of orthodoxy or inviting their myopic views. Let us examine the definition of Islam in the broadest possible terms and see if it makes any logical sense in today's society. The word 'Islam' is said to mean submission, surrender, perhaps alignment and integration with. ---

Submit, surrender or align with what, and why?

Take any action as an example; be it an act of *thought, word* or *deed.* Every act must submit to a logic, plan or scheme for it to make sense, or be called a meaningful pursuit. Unplanned behaviour is aimless and unpredictable and may not achieve any result, except perhaps destruction or negation of order — that which some planned or coherent action is trying to establish. One may however say, that this too is a pursuit; but destruction is generally not accepted as a viable purpose. It is perhaps a negation of the very concept of a purposeful action. A purpose is progressive and forward bound, where as negation is annihilating in its approach. We thus infer that, submission must also make some logical sense and should have a purpose to be viable and generally acceptable. Now, submission itself becomes a voluntary act if one's awareness and knowledge support its reason and logic.

The whole exercise of '*being*' must have had a motive, for otherwise, it becomes a meaningless farce. Now, for the fulfillment of any motive, some tools, means or implements are essential. In the case of human beings these means may be mental , verbal or physical in nature. Thoughts are mental tools, language and words are verbal aids and actions are means of physical expression. To elaborate and explain it a little more, let us say that, to praise or curse someone one needs thoughts and /or words -- which are the tools for accomplishing the desired act. And, to physically help or harm someone one needs appropriate tools to do the job. Now again, the tools and implements must be functional, within ones control and must somehow relate to the task. For example to kiss someone lips would be a more appropriate tool then legs. The latter, though also a tool and perhaps functional, would be more appropriate to implant a good kick instead. Again, the tools or implements one chooses must perform well and efficiently to accomplish the task, or they will either be modified or replaced. The tools must also obey and serve the master.

Each one of us has some natural tools and some others one can improvise. The personal tools would be the parts of ones body -- arms, legs, eyes, heart, liver etc. Some of which are external and some internal. Some work under the control of ones free- will, and some function autonomously, under natural laws. Each part of the body has a specific function that it performs dutifully and efficiently according to its nature and structure. All things that function and perform their naturally assigned tasks are called '*Muslim*' as they obey and submit to the laws that govern them, that is, the laws of Nature. In nature, everything obeys these natural laws and cannot deviate from them. Humans however, have a unique position in this regard. They have the extra quality of a 'free- will' ; which becomes pronounced with development in age and sense. This free-will is an inherent human quality and comes from the fact that they have evolved as a species and have reached a high level in Nature's design of things. The free will is human being's most distinguishing attribute. It can be put to use with the aid of the mind and its power of reasoning. How one uses this free- will is the real test of ones ability to discipline and control one's other faculties and their function, those that he/ she has in common with other living things. E.g. hunger, self-preservation, need for shelter, love and hate etc. etc. The faculties therefore, too, are also all Muslims because they all submit and perform the assigned tasks competently and diligently under the laws that control them – the system of free-will of a person.

So what is the purpose of human beings?

If the definition of Muslim, given above is understood, then to begin with, every person is a born Muslim, because at that stage one is completely under the control of *Nature* and its laws and dutifully submits to them. One does not have a developed sense or free-will and in fact very limited independence. Notably, a human baby is more helpless than the offspring of other creatures, and remains so for a relatively longer period. Even here there is a logic, but we will deal with that some other time perhaps. The thing to note however, is, that this most helpless of creatures eventually becomes the most powerful, and perhaps the most useful in the scheme of *Nature's* evolutionary process. At the present stage of evolution humans have gained the ability to be aware and also be able to participate in *Nature's* own scheme of things. Every thing thus seems to have a purpose and value on the scale of *Nature's* balance. In fact human beings can aid in it and even promote certain natural processes by virtue of their intellect and consequent overall superiority. This may sound as an ode to ourselves, but which other creature has the ability to write an ode to itself, or for that matter even read and write on its own.

The higher up on the scale of evolution the creature is, the more the awareness it has, and can understand both its own rights and obligations. *As evolution progresses and reaches the stage of self-perpetuation, it becomes self-participating and self-directing as well. For, if it is not so the result would be self-destructing and self-diminishing.* Now the tendency of self-destruction in an evolving system is a negative or detrimental trait, and does not serve the logic of its very existence. Humans are also a part of this self-perpetuating system and are positioned at a very high level in the whole spectrum of evolution -- whereby they have gained the capability of being conscious of the system itself. They may not fully appreciate or understand the purpose of the system of which they are a part, yet they are aware of it and know that such a structure exists. They probe and search for its meaning in every thing around them. They do this by the use of their most important and uniquely individualistic tool – the mind. This mind however, like every thing else, is a double-edged sword. It is both positive and negative. It is both creative and destructive. It has the power to both accept or reject. This in turn, depends on the basis of the thought itself, and ones approach to the subject. If the basis or origination of thought or conscious analysis is positivism and open mindedness, it will endow progressive and constructive results. But if the idea takes birth in doubt and deceit it will promote negativity and resistance to progress. Let us take an example. The splitting of a heavy atom (fission), or joining two small atoms (fusion), releases tremendous energy. This release of power can be utilised either constructively, e.g. to generate electricity; or destructively, e.g. to make a bomb. Interestingly enough, however, the process for electrical power generation is based on the principle of a controlled and balanced nuclear reaction; whereas a bomb is uncontrolled release of energy. This points to the fact that progressive processes are usually harnessed, balanced and controlled activities. Uncontrolled reactions can be catastrophic.

We have now come to a stage where we can understand what it means by — 'to submit, surrender and align with'. It is really, *Nature*, and its process of self-propagation and perpetuation which is to be accepted, submitted to and participated in. *One who consciously does so, with a belief that there is such a thing as a Natural system with its supreme laws and submits, is a consciously believing Muslim;* and one who denies it, is not. Questioning, probing, fathoming and then accepting natural phenomena are all Muslim traits. Our tasks as humans is then to study, explore, understand, align and harness the progressive aspects of the Laws of 'Cause and Effect'; in other words to correctly use ones personal and or improvised tools towards the furthering and promoting, not only of the self, but of the system as a whole. Is this not alignment with the 'Laws of Nature'?. These Laws are the frame work under which *Nature* Itself operates and accomplishes the process of change and evolution.

Human beings are perhaps at such a stage of evolutionary development where they are now, themselves, consciously participating in the functioning of the system. See the capability of human endeavour that has brought it to the stage of self-replication through the advancement of scientific knowledge and techniques – cloning, for example. Genetic know how has been firmly established in the genetic engineering of food, animals and medicine. Robotics and electronics are two other fields being rapidly developed. All these processes have remarkable potentials for equipping human beings with some of the most powerful tools yet imagined. As a consequence they are able to perform deeds that were so far unimaginable – cloning, space travel etc. etc.

Why do we do what we do, and where will all this curiosity, quest and effort lead to? This is the age old question of -- Who we are, and why we are what we are?

The purpose of human existence cannot be the all 'here and now', -- or as it has been said, " Eat, drink and be merry, for tomorrow you die". Notice, that every Now (which is also known as present) was once out There (that is also called the future), and will eventually become a Then (which is the past); and so the natural cycle of life continues to churn. This is how time is spent, and with it, all human effort. Or to say it another way; -- time and effort seem to recede or deplete. In a way they go back. Now, according to the laws of Physics and so also of Nature – 'to every action there is an equal and opposite reaction'. Hence, if time and every thing connected with it goes in a certain direction, something should come out of it as the 'effect of that cause', and would proceed in the opposite direction. The outcome of this decrease in time, etc. is the increase in knowledge and/ or awareness. In other words there is a price to be paid for every thing. In yet another way, gain in awareness is the return of ones investment of time and effort. This way of utilizing the resource of time and effort can also be called the 'consummation of self '. This may not be a monetary gain, but believe me it is worth much more. One thing that comes out of all human activity is the unveiling and expanding of new vistas of vision i.e. the furthering of knowledge. Every step in physical, mental and spiritual advancement is basically the increase of awareness and knowledge which consequently leads to 'self-growth' and further evolution.

Now, having borne with the logic so far, let us take the next step.

All stable systems in nature have one thing in common -- they are all balanced and are evolving. A controlled evolutionary change, as said above, is perhaps more enduring and longer lasting than a violent revolutionary one. Observe both the macrocosm and the microcosm. The solar system maintains its stability because it is balanced and evolving. At the other end of the spectrum of the Cosmos, the classical atomic structure follows the same principle of balance and poise. We thus infer that balance and evolution are not only the keys to a successful life they are also its basic principle. The greater the dawn of awareness, the greater the attainment of balance and, the more the elevation of poise. Sages, Monks, Sadhus and perhaps Prophets are a set of people that demonstrate this. They seem to be that group of individuals who have harnessed the tumult of material desires and mental agitations and reached the balance of mind, body and soul, to acquire the poise of serenity. They are evolved souls who have reached the next level of holonic hierarchy. They would surely be a holon level higher than common human beings. Their next step would be the *holon* of Universal Spirit, where all souls integrate and acquire the oneness with *Nature* itself, perhaps, the final stage of the great Holarchy. — *The Spirit.* [3]

We have now reached that stage of our discussion where we can perhaps

---

3   I am not using the word 'God' intentionally, because, (a) it restricts the mind to an over all reverential Being, that supposedly predetermines everything, thus confusing the issue of free-will and reward and punishment. (b) A psychological barrier is imposed on the free flow of thought for examining fresh ideas and beliefs.

appreciate the fact that submission, surrender and conscious willingness are the only ways and means to align with the dictates of Nature and the Natural Law in order to progress. This will perhaps, not only unveil the secrets of those Laws, but in turn alleviate the Self to a level of awareness where the *Created* can look at the *Face of the Creator* and admire His/ Her work.

This, in a nut shell perhaps, is the essence of being a Muslim, and the broad teachings of Islam as seen in a contemporary light.

Chapter Thirteen
THE RELEVANCE OF QUR'AN IN THE 21ST CENTURY

Whether Qur'an is relevant or not in the 21st century will begin to make more sense if we study the relevance of religion in our lives and the nature of the Book itself.

It is not only the West that has a distorted image of Islam, most Muslims have it too. This is due primarily to the reliance on the orthodox fundamentalist's interpretation of it. Now, the common Muslim is as simple and naive as the common Christian, Jew or for that matter a follower of any other religion. Each one is absorbed in their day-to-day pursuits of basic survival, without much time and inclination for complexities. One seeks some peace and solace in religion but finds no remedy in the orthodox preaching and the mundane sermons from the pulpit. Most fundamentalist preaching tends to take one back instead of forward in both time and ideas, and so most worshipers perform their routine rituals without ever reflecting on the meaning and reason for them.

All monotheistic religions preach a similar end and that is— *'Submission to the Will of the Creator'*. If submission is willing and conscious it results in attainment of harmony with Nature. If unwilling and unconscious, the result is the agony of conflict. Every religion aims at the uplift of man and the basic axioms of all religions are the same. For, none preaches loot and plunder, none teaches to kill or maim. Each tries to channelize the animal nature of man for the common good of humanity. Islam too promotes these values. Islamic philosophy is geared towards the understanding of ones 'Self', and suggests measures for self- correction, both in relation to other human beings and to *Nature* Itself. The greatest flaw in the fundamentalist's approach to Islam is that they preach that there is only one solution to any problem, and that all solutions are recipes in The Book.

A closer review of The Qur'an, however, shows that it is a classic and a book of knowledge based on:

1. Lessons from Historical episodes

2. Guidelines for legal framework, and

3. A *Philosophy* of life.

It will continue to be a classic and a book for all times if it is studied as such. If it is taken as a black and white prescription for all ills, it will at times, be used out of context; for then, the book will be found to contradict itself, and will be discredited and eventually discarded. As the changing of times is a dynamic process, events of today cannot be explained by the facts of yesterday alone.

It is inbuilt in the nature of man to enquire, seek and find. When all else fails and his own efforts have been exhausted, one turns to mother *Nature*, which in its classical fundamental form is known as *God* or the *Deity*. The answer, is in fact, revealed by one's own *Inner-self*, or if you wish to call it, the *Over-self*, as in the end both are the extension of the same *Self*. The answers can come in a number of ways. The solution may appear in a dream. There may be a flash of intuition. One may make autosuggestion to oneself. These again, may either be conscious, those, which one is fully aware of and are based on one's rational thoughts; or unconscious, whereby the hidden idea comes to the surface like a bubble rising from within the depths of oneself -- in a, hitherto, inexplicable manner. This is the same form in which the deepest of thinkers like sages, prophets and men of spiritual elevation get their knowledge and wisdom.

As this form of release of information is still commonly unfathomed, and is not completely rationalized, it is usually pushed in the background and not readily accepted. Modern science is making much effort in the study of the functioning of the brain and the mind and will perhaps come up with some plausible explanation of this phenomenon also. This uncontrolled and unconscious enlightenment has been termed as *revelation*. The strength of revelation depends on ones depth of desire and honesty of purpose. Such means of communication have been established only by a few –- called the enlightened ones -- those who have fathomed the means to tap into the mysterious *'Cosmic Consciousness'*, and perhaps understand its message. To attain this level of rapport with the *Source* one has to liberate oneself from the mundane traps of physical hindrances and become able to communicate with the deepest of one's inner depths. It is said, all knowledge seems to lie buried within, and has to be exposed and brought to a conscious level by a concerted, laborious and painstaking process of disciplining oneself for self -exploration and self- discovery. The Qur'an itself says:

**O man, you have to strive and go on striving towards
your Lord, then will you meet Him** (84:6)

Primarily, the Qur'an seems to be a monologue of the *Creator* -- either with Its messenger, or through him with others. Its revelations reflect the

<u>*thought process* of the prophet.</u> When It addresses the votary directly, It does so in the form of autosuggestions. It gives him advice, direction, assurance, and sometimes, even reprimand. It seems to provide answers to questions the Prophet sought, either explicitly or implicitly. Revealing to him truths of episodes of historical significance and the happenings with other prophets, their experiences and their handlings of various situations, and the doings of human beings in general. It suggests solutions for a variety of circumstances and explains the principles behind many of them. Of greatest importance is the Universal philosophy of the Qur'an and its overall worldview, encompassing not only the earth and the heavens but also all that lies between them. The Prophet derived knowledge and instruction from the Qur'an, practiced its preaching, and thus, in fact seemed to have lived it in its entirety. This is because the personality that received and perceived the message was an impeccably honest, forthright and a righteous individual with the welfare of humanity at heart. He was thus unique in his own thought process. Only he could have had a complete understanding of how, when and why those thoughts came to him. Now therefore, only the prophet could have lived the Qur'an in its entirety. All the rest of us can only make our individual effort to fathom his thought process to the level of our own understanding and knowledge of it, and then try to emulate it.

An all-encompassing theory would remain current even with the passage of time. It should be dynamic and be able to explain situations within its existing laws. Only a Natural theory is such a vehicle. The religious idea based on this natural theory can be ever current and practicable at all times, because it is based on the axioms of nature. This is what Islam is. It is a dynamic philosophy because it preaches the understanding, aligning and adherence to the dictates of the laws of '*Cause* and *Effect*'.

You must be dying to ask the question that—'If this is so, why are

Muslims so miserable and down trodden in the world?' The only answer to that is that they do not understand their own religion and do not make individual effort to study and explore its essence, or promote those of its values that are compatible with the current time and age. They have either forgotten the gist of the message or had never understood it in the first place. On the other hand, primarily people of Western cultures are seen to have understood, accepted and adopted the basics of these natural Laws, and are using them for making remarkable material progress. They may not have realized the spiritual significance of the causes and their effects and remain primarily the level of physical gains. Muslims mostly listen to Qur'anic preaching through second hand sermons and deliverances, some repeat it verbatim, but only few ever read the message and think for themselves. Some of the many reasons for shying away from the Qur'an and its contents are:

a. It has been unnaturally sanctified and preserved in the niche. This over reverential treatment of the Book has dissuaded people from it and they postpone consulting it at the moment of need, because they have been petrified of touching it unceremoniously. .

b. Its main purpose, as a book of common reference, has been restricted to the hands of the orthodoxy and their interpretation of it is unquestioningly accepted. Its explanation is supposed to be their sacred duty alone.

c. These orthodox, in their own ignorance or fear, promote more awe than reason, thereby distorting the actual and real purpose of the Book.

d. It is read only in the letter and its spirit is hardly pondered upon or understood. The Qur'an is a classic and has to be deeply probed. Are not most classics read over and over again to be fully understood and appreciated? E.g. To fully appreciate Shakespeare do we not study the history of his time. So why not for Qur'an?

e. It is mainly taught to children, and that in most cases, in a language so foreign to them that they do not understand a word of it and are repelled. Any repulsion at that young age is rather deep rooted and requires a real effort to overcome. This naturally builds a resistance to return to it.

f. Since it has never been popularized as a book of knowledge, only half-baked translations of it are available. Those done by scholars and liberated individuals have been shunned and made redundant. All this is so because the hegemony of the ' mullah' reigns supreme, and it is not in his interest to educate the ignorant masses, perhaps because his own short sight holds him back.

g. Last but not the least, the book if ever consulted, is mostly done for its legal framework pronouncements alone, and those too applied only in letter, their spirit or philosophy is hardly ever perceived or accepted. Little or no thought is given to conditions pertaining over fourteen hundred years ago, and the dictates of those laws are thought to be applicable in totality in the present. The Qur'an's philosophy and its human psychology, which are far deeper, more elaborate and perhaps more relevant, are hardly ever probed, debated upon and propagated.

The whole foregone scenario of mishandling and misunderstanding of the Book has come about over centuries of inattention and disregard for liberated intellectual enquiry. This was inbred in the Muslim psyche by vested interests of close-minded propagators of status quo, those who took up the guardianship of the religion. Some of who lead the ignorant through their own ignorance, others by politicizing and exploiting the message to suit their fancy. Remove these shortcomings from the study of Qur'an and the relevance of the Book, not only for the twenty first century, but all times, will become clearly visible. Consider it as a classic presented in an admirably rich language, and indeed it will be treated as another landmark in human thought. Remember classics are for all time, and so would be the Qur'an.

The Qur'an, if seen in rational terms, takes on a completely new meaning, and the whole narration becomes the invaluable insight of a genius. That, Prophet Muhammad was one, becomes evident if his message is studied with logic and rational composure, and not with unbridled emotion and undue devotion -- that which is inculcated by blind rituals and empty porous traditions. For, unrestrained and uncontrolled reverence in the form of an over cautious and awe inspiring approach to the Qur'an, and the personality of its presenter, leads to undue restriction on the flow of balanced thought and the questions that arise there from. On the other hand judging it on hearsay or drawing-room pseudo intellectuality is no less reprehensible. Rationality, which is the order of the day, demands that the Book be approached from a new and liberated angle, that which is in keeping with the dictates of the present time and age. Keeping the message shackled in thousand-year-old chains and restricting its use, has rusted it beyond recognition. Its original purpose and meaning has got cluttered in politicizing and over zealous religious interpretation. There is no need to change or alter the message or any part thereof, as that would constitute intellectual dishonesty and unpardonable distortion. The only thing needed is to explore it's meaning from a different angle and a balanced coherent approach, in consonance with the times.

The Qur'an, therefore, is a guidance for anyone who wishes to study the workings of the nature of man and his surroundings, and the understandings of the laws of ' *Cause* and *Effect*' as deciphered by the prophet. Once the working of these laws is fathomed, the nature of *Nature* Itself becomes comprehensible. For, *Nature* is the originator of all systems and laws that govern each and everything—even *Itself*. It may be said that God's alone is the perfect system, and systematic perfection leads to godliness.

Besides all of the above the relevance of the Qur'an has its support in the fact that:

(a). If the Qur'an is the basis of faith of over 1.3 billion Muslims of the world, it surely must have some relevance.

(b). If the Qur'an is a classic then it must make an impression on man and his education, and so it surely must have some relevance.

(c). If the Qur'an can be motivational of its followers to lay down their lives for it and it's preaching, would it not have relevance?

(d). If the Qur'an can keep this august gathering, and so many others besides, engrossed in debating and analyzing it, the Book must have some relevance.

There would be many more arguments that can be presented in this context but the above should suffice to establish the point.

It has been a tradition of mine to close with a verse of Ghalib, who is one of the most metaphorical poet philosophers of Urdu language. If you can detect the metaphor in the verse in relation to the Quran, you may be on the road to the key to the metaphors of the Qur'an itself.

Nazara kea hareef hoe ous barq e husan ka
Josh e bahar jalvae koe jis kay naqaab hai

137

What spectacle can claim rivalry,
Of that ray of beauteous glow.
Whose effulgence is veiled,
By the springs exuberant show.

(My paraphrase of the verse is that: If you substitute the word ' spectacle' with the word ' classic'—as any classic is a spectacle of human endeavour —then the meaning of the first stanza of the verse becomes:

Which ' classic' can match the Qur'an—in beauty of language, diction, poetry, content etc.

Replace the word ' veil' with ' protect or guard or save'—because all this is in the nature of the veil—then the meaning of the second stanza of the verse would be:

That the glory, strength or power of the Creator Itself will preserve it.

This contention is verifiable by the Qur'an itself. (15:9)

Chapter Fourteen

THE NATURE OF A NATURAL DEITY

A broad minded approach is presently needed for looking at some of the most common topics from a new and contemporary angle. And it is this that is required to examine old beliefs and dogmatic religious ideas in the present and changed conditions.

If *God* were to be incarcerated in a cage, He would at best be able to pace up and down like a lion in the zoo. This is exactly the state most religious fundamentalist thoughts have accomplished. They have created an anthropomorphic *Deity* and given *It* the attributes they could think of, for *Him*, themselves. Their God loves because they can feel love. Their God gets angry too. This again is so because they themselves know of anger. Their God is benevolent and merciful because that is what they wish Him to be. Then their God also forgives. This again is so because they know that it is human nature to falter and learn from mistakes and if there is no forgiveness there will not be a second chance to try again. Yet again, their God even punishes. This attribute is needed to be given to God to keep the wavering humanity in line and on a desired path. The concept of reward and punishment is essential and gives the effect of the carrot and the stick -- all in keeping with human nature. So each succeeding religious idea adjusted its concept of God and modified His image as according to what was felt fit or necessary to suit the circumstance.

The polytheists started with each attribute being represented by a separate deity. Over the ages this showed shortcomings and an amalgamation took place and monotheism was reborn. Here all attributes were combined to say that God is Omnipotent, Omnipresent, All- seeing and All- knowing. He is also described as the Uncaused Cause, the Unmoved Mover, the Completely Un-needful and finally the *'Immanently Indispensable'*. Each one of these definitions would hold some truth as each statement is associated with people of enlightenment, wisdom and Universal standing. Examining the last one, 'The Immanently Indispensable', seems to bring one closest to the Universal nature of the Omnipotent Eternal Being. Immanently Indispensable in simple terms means the 'inherent necessity', the innate essence without which a thing cannot exist; for without God nothing would have been possible or come into being.

There are two ways of controlling or governing a thing, either from the outside or from within. Whereas, exterior control would need accessories or additional tools to exert the power, internal control on the other hand, would require the presence of the controller within the system itself. Being within the system and part of it the *Controller* would not only know its condition first hand, s/he could also take immediate corrective measures. However, in the method of internal control the Controller would itself be affected by the change and would also have to follow the laws that govern the entire system. But in the externally controlled method the controller is above and beyond the principles which apply to the system, and may not be affected by the change taking place in or on the system.

We shall now try to examine and see if the Deity we are studying is an external *Controller*, as per the commonly understood and propagated religious pronouncements, or is in effect an integral part of the *Creation* itself.

Were '*It*' to be an external manipulator *It* would not be affected by the doings and actions of the created entity. Well! What then is the reason and need for the creation itself? Is it just to sit and observe the unfurling of the scenario from a distance and enjoy the ups and downs of the constituents, and manipulate them at whim? If so, then for what purpose? This, in some ways, is a rather rudimentary and meaningless approach. For, if an act is performed without a reason or motive it is an exercise in futility. Hence everything connected with creation and creativity would lose all meaning, and God would assume the role of a puppeteer. Now, as any human activity is not without a purpose, why then would the Creator act outside the line of meaning and reason? This mode of reasoning may seem very human and anthropomorphic in itself. Yet, is it possible for humans to have and share ideas besides a human way of expressing and sharing them?

Having raised so many questions, let us try and find some answers.

It is said that 'beauty lies in the eyes of the beholder'. Were there no beholder there would be no beauty, and were there no beauty no beholder would be needed. The one is the essence of the other. If the beholder were to shut his eyes would beauty cease to exist? According to one school of philosophy it would. Yet, it would perhaps exist, but both the beauty and the beholder would be unconscious or unaware of each other and thus be unaffected by each. Only awareness gives meaning to things. The effect of a thing makes it presence felt, and the presence of a thing gives it the effect. It takes two to tango. The Creator would be nothing without the created, and the creation would have been meaningless if it did not impart any effect or influence on the Creator Itself.

A simple statement can have profound significance. For instance, 'Any and everything anyone does, does so for their self'. It sounds quite selfish, but seen in a non-material sense it gives an axiomatic connotation. The *Self* cannot be separated from *Itself*, however much one tries. The Sadhu, Sufi and Saint may be able to detach their-self from themselves but they remain attached to the *Over-Self*, which is nothing but another dimension of Self. Once again, a deed may be completely unselfish yet its very performance yields some or other form of effect or influence on either of the Selves.

Ghalib, the famous poet philosopher of India in the nineteenth century, has described this so aptly, in the context of piety, when he says:

Kaya zuhud ko manoon keh neh hoe garchay rayayee
Padash e amal ki tama khaam bohat hai

Why piety should I acclaim?
It may well have no worldly show.
To gain is the aim of every act,
However pious it be, though.

Having thus established a premise that behind every motive there is a motive, what then is the motive of the *One* who has created all motives?

The answer to the question would lie in the fact that there has got to be a reason for the entire hullabaloo of creation and creativity. This raises the next question -- that of *purpose*. Now, this is more profound and each individual will approach it differently and examine the idea from his/ her own frame of reference. The approach here is that if 'purpose' is the essential element in the argument, then purpose is what should be sought. Before answering this it will be essential to establish what could be the needs of 'One' Who has everything and Who is in complete control of all. As done earlier, we have to borrow a line from religion to pursue this course. Remember, we are told that 'Man' is made in the image of 'God', so if we were to study the nature of *'man'* it should give some inkling to the nature of the *'Deity'* Itself. For such a *'Being'* to do what It does, it would have to be *'Self-generated'* and hence *'Self-centred'*. We draw this inference by reflecting on the actions of humans who are in a relatively comfortable and a comparatively self-contained category in the world, and see what motivates them to action. For instance, what would be the motivation of leaders, sages, philosophers and the like? Power, and the desire for it may motivate leaders. Tranquility, and the quest of peace may be the search of the sage; and love of knowledge and the quest for truth may work for the philosophers. Each and everyone, however, has to spend time and energy, or in other words *'consume oneself'*, in the pursuit of the desire. The act of self-consummation is the only way that may lead to achievement. For, to get a reaction there has to be some action first. The feeling of achievement of a constructive act is known as *'fulfillment of self'*.

If One has got the means and power to do things, the main motivation would be to try and test the limit of one's ability and improve upon them. Now, where the ability itself is limitless, the quest would be to seek *awareness* of the process and the reason for this ability. The Deity, therefore, having all else in the bag, is seeking to become *aware* of *Itself*. To see how and why 'It does what It does'. For, when It says 'Be' ! a thing 'Becomes' (Al Qur'an 36:82). *The instant the Deity gets the thought as to How and Why a thing becomes what It wishes it to be, i.e. the moment the Deity begins to question Its own inherent nature of creation and its own Creativity, It takes the step forward from being an Unconscious Creator to One Who wants to be Conscious and Aware of Its-Self -- or an Unfulfilled Deity starts to seek Self Fulfilment;* or so to say that the Deity, which has this power to issue a command and get instant gratification, would seek to get awareness of Its own inherent qualities. In other words an *'Unconscious Deity'*, capable of doing what It wishes to do, is seeking to become a *'Consciously Conscious Being'; studying the 'cause and effect' of It's own acts. For, only then will It accomplish Self-fulfillment.* This It will do by going through the entire process of **'*Re-becoming Itself*'**, in order to recognize *It's* own Self and thereby fulfill Its own purpose -- much like the activity that all of humanity is engaged in, i.e. seeking the reason of their own being and the purpose of their lives. *By re-enacting the play the Deity is going to gain full awareness of its own actions and, in the process the reason for them. To do this It will have to replicate Itself from scratch, and become aware of the process of becoming everything starting from nothing.* It seems to start with 'the Big Bang'—goes through the phase of expansion, condensation, reformation, compression and subsequent evolution modes, to eventually reach 'the Big Crunch' perhaps. (using the terms of Astrophysics).

This, *self-reformation of Self*, is the building of a *System* by the *Natural Deity* whereby the whole process may be re-enacted on its own, under its *self-sufficient* and *self-subservient* laws.

And this gives an interesting foundation upon which the whole idea of this essay is based.

All three monotheistic religions subscribe to the idea that the 'Kosmos' manifested in stages or days – 6 to be exact. (Note that Kosmos as opposed to Cosmos, according to Holonistic theory, is the cumulative outcome of all creation. It encompasses all matter, energy, psychology and their interplay in the entire Creativity.)

Again let's borrow some lines from religion to see how it all started.

It is God who created the heavens and the earth
and all that lies between them,
in six spans, then assumed all authority.

You have no protector other than Him,

nor any intercessor.

Will you not be warned even then?

(Al Qur'an 32 : 4)

AND

Surely your Lord is God

who created the heavens and the earth

in six spans of time,

then assumed all power.

He covers up the day with night which comes

chasing it fast;

and the sun and moon and the stars

are subject to His command.

It is His to create and enjoin.

Blessed be God,

the Lord of all the worlds.

(Al Qur'an 7:54)

The concept of *spans* of time is superior to *days,* as given by some religious accounts. This is so because the mention of days usually restricts one's thought to the common conception of a day, i.e. 24 hours. Spans on the other hand brings to mind a period of time, not limited to 24 hours; as some phenomena must surely have taken a relatively longer period than others to accomplish and sustain. The narration of the Qur'an certainly seems more profound and evolved, and shows a greater depth and maturity of intellect. Further, *'assumed all power'* is once again an indication of a more

145

developed concept than *"And on the seventh day God rested."* For surely the Deity is no earthling to be in need of rest due to depletion of energy after hard labour, or the likes of it.

These *Six Spans* (or 6 days as mentioned in some religions) refer to the 6 phases through which creation and its development took place. It changed, matured or evolved till it finally reached the human state. From there on it takes up the mode or capability of self-development and eventual *self-replication* and then the *re-merger* into the *Source*. Note that man is learning or becoming conscious of himself by the same progression of self-replication as Nature.

These six stages could be *Nature's* own mechanism of transformation from Ex-nihilo {*Nothingness* – zero (0)} to {*Everythingness* or infinity (0)}, and thus getting a close awareness of the emergence of a *Self- perpetuating* system—which the Deity Itself is.

These six spans or stages may well be:

(1). The stage of *Ex-Nihilo, Nothingness, Zero, Unawareness*. This is the stage when the Deity is Un-exposed, Self-contained or Dormant—not that It lacked anything or was short of completion as a Creative Power, but that It did not fathom Its own power, and had yet not become *conscious* of *Its* own capabilities, and was thus *unfulfilled*.

Another way to explain this is through the example of the relationships of 'potential' and 'kinetic' energies. Potential energy is energy at rest. Kinetic energy on the other hand is dynamic energy. When the potential energy changes to dynamic, work gets done. Another way to see this is levels. When two terminals of a battery are connected current can begin to flow from higher potential level to the lower level of potential and as a result some work can be done. Again water can flow from a higher level to a lower level and if channelized through turbines work can be done. The work that *Nature* does is to perform the *Act of Creation* i.e, bringing forth from nothingness to everythingness.

(2). The stage of pure *Idea* or potential *energy*. A *subconscious* state in which *Nature* is in Its basic condition of *pure thought* and is as yet stationary—static—potential , not yet dynamic.

(3). The phase of *conversion* of pure Energy or idea, into *matter* as per 'E=mc2'—The coming forth of the Cosmos (the material Universe), the *Earth* and all *Non-living* matter.

(4). The stage of the *interaction* of dynamic Energy with Matter—The origination of the cellular process and the emergence of *Static Living things*—Vegetation and sedentary life—say '*the matter-energy conglomerate*'.

(5). The stage or progress by *evolution*. The incorporation of mobility, and development of *animal life*, the final stage of which is *Man (or human)*

(6). The development of the *human mind* with the incorporation of *psychological processes* in the hitherto underdeveloped animal brain. This is the journey humanity takes through the various phases of development by trial and error. It conquers ignorance by knowledge and awareness, attaining self- advancement unto the achievement of the level of the stage of *re-merger*. This is the level when 'matter-energy conglomerate' would have acquired the capability to convert back to pure *Energy*, and then to *pure form* or *pure thought*. This is thus the stage of re-attainment of *the Original Form*. The position when the *Deity* has become aware of *Itself* through knowledge acquired by humans – the instrument created by *It* for that specific purpose. Man is thus the final vehicle in *Nature's* process of acquiring *Self- awareness* and thus *Self-fulfillment* through regeneration by *Self-replication,* or the process of *reverse-engineering Itself.*

(7). The Day or the stage or phase when re-merger occurs. This is when *Nothingness* becomes *Everythingness,* and *Everything* becomes *Nothing.* The *Deity* achieves full awareness of *Itself.* The Parts and the Whole become One. The stage when Zero attains Infinity. Or 0 ☒☒ (Notice that zero '0' when it repeats itself, or makes a full reverse cycle it becomes infinity (☒); Or when one zero fuses with another zero it becomes infinite. Infinity is when one nothingness is interwoven with another nothingness.)

And finally:

"Surely we are from God
to Him we shall return".

(Al Qur'an 2:156)

To fulfill this religious prophecy, the Zero (man) must move forward and merge with another Zero (God) to complete the cyclical Zeros, i.e. Infinity. For, *'without God man is nothing,* and *without man God is dormant or unaware* of *Itself.'* Both are the essentials in the equation *of AWARENESS of meaningful EXISTENCE.*

Once again let's take a pointer form Ghalib and see how he saw a similar concept in his own unique way:

Na tha kutch to Khuda tha
Kutch na hoota to Khuda hoota
Dubooya mujh ko honay nay
Na hoota main to kaya hoota

When naught existed, God existed.
Had none there been, God would be.
<u>My own existence lowered me.</u>
Would I not be, what would it be?

However, I question this line of reasoning, and if and when I meet Ghalib I will ask him why he did not write thus:

Na tha kutch to Khuda tha,
Kutch na hoota to Khuda hoota
<u>-Sujhaya- mujh ko honay nay,</u>
na hota main to Kaya hoota?

(For if I had not been brought forth I would no doubt have been part of the whole; but an insensitive, unconscious, ignorant part. My very being and individual existence gives me an identity of an entity and is responsible for making me aware of that fact.) Hence:

When naught existed God existed,
Had none there been, God would be.
My very being, this made me see.
Would I not be, what would it be?

The next thing to look at is how the *'Natural Deity'* harnesses Its own nature.

Were the 'Natural Deity' to be an uncontrolled Force or Energy, It would not accomplish anything but destruction. This is not likely, for if it were so then why the elaborate process of Creation and the 'apparent systematic evolution' of it? For, to do any worthwhile thing an act has to be thought out, planned and then executed; keeping the three – thought, plan, and action in harmony and balanced along the way. Nature Itself demonstrates and achieves this by exercising *Self-subservience* and maintaining *It's* own *Self-control* through *Self-discipline*. Having the idea and laying down a plan of action *It* executes it by taking *Itself* along the route of *Self-nurture*, obeying *It's* own laid down rules and regulations along the way. *Self-restraint* is implemented by *Self-sacrifice*, i.e. voluntarily surrendering and placing *Its* own 'Self' subservient to *It's* own laid down principles. Were *It* not to do this and somehow act outside of those laws, *It* would negate Its own *Supreme -Sublimity* and *Purity* -- for then *It* would be adopting shortcuts in *It's* own proposed goal of true *Self-education* and subsequent *Self- fulfillment*. *It* would then, not be able to establish a method or system to facilitate and promote *It's* creation to achieve the level of *Self-regeneration* -- which humans seem to be geared to do. Also going the easy way would refute the claim that, ' *Truth is the basis of all Natural laws and must prevail in the end'*. It just goes to show that *truth* is really honesty with oneself, as *Nature Itself* demonstrates. This fact may be further understood by examining the real nature of truth as seen through human perspective. Self-understanding, self-analysing and then believing and accepting one's beliefs is really what truth is. When one questions, deciphers, then understands and accepts the reasoning and logic of one's own explanation of facts and data, it becomes one's truth. As each one is unique and an individual, hence each one has a unique way of understanding and accepting an idea and therefore, each one has his/ her own truth. Every one's Truth is thus relative to another's. Absolute truth is beyond the domain of this world and may exist in another paradigm.

Let us view this another way. *Nature*, which is capable of everything, does imply Self- restraint even in situations where it is well within Its power to affect change instantaneously. *It* does not interfere in the workings of *It's* own System and its Laws, and lets the process take its due course to bring about the desired effect. *It* lets the cycle of things be completed in their own natural period of incubation. For example, it is well within *Nature's* ability to annihilate and destroy a person who, say is blasphemous and openly curses God and flouts His laws. Were *Nature* to be the anthropomorphic God of the religious thought, there would surely be a show of anger with an immediate reprimand or annihilation of the sacrilegious being. But no, the *Natural Deity* let's events take their course, and treats the offence according to the laws of *'cause* and *effect'*. The offender's perverted thinking and unbridled free will, either makes him/her repent, and this repentance becomes the penance and subsequent cure for wrong thoughts. Or otherwise, the course of action of the offender takes him/her along a path of doings that are naturally detrimental to progress or success and s/he meets his/her own natural doom -- maybe by openly hurting a believer's feelings and getting beaten up in return.

The resultant effect of the cause may or may not be discernible in the span of one's *material life*, yet its repercussions are carried forward and borne by that part of human existence which survives into the future, which may well be what we call *'Soul'* or the *reincarnation* of it. Now, this would make logical sense only if existence is seen as extending beyond the usually visible span of *birth, life* and *death*. There must surely be existence before birth and so also after the occurrence of physical death, because most natural phenomena are continuous and connected, so why not life. Look at it another way, and that is that a *human* is nothing but an infinitesimal extension of *Nature Itself*, which is surely continuous and goes from the past, through the present, and into the future. Physical life is perhaps that portion of being which we can discern by our limited sensory perception -- a tool, mainly given to us for this phase of life.

Each individual that passes on to the next stage of existence takes along some *experience, exposure* and *awareness* of the life s/he has lived, and leaving behind some effect on the material world that remains behind. The sum total of every individual's past experiences, exposures and awareness add up into the store house of *Nature Itself,* and enriches *It's* Own data bank, so to say, and gives to *It* the cumulative meaning of all perceptions and actions in the Kosmos. *Nature thus takes a giant leap forward with each single step of mankind.* As said elsewhere, (in the other essay …Ultimate Human Reach)

While it is humanly impossible to tame all the information of a given moment and manipulate it to affect destiny, it may be possible by some Divine Entity to do so. And again, only by that Divinity which is 'immanently indispensable' and is the inherent necessity of all things and everything; because It is being individually affected by the doings of all humanity separately, as well as collectively, and is Itself affecting everyone of It's creation in It's turn. It is getting full awareness, consciousness and knowledgeable of all happenings, all the time. This is how a Natural Deity would shape human destiny and thus also It's own.

The *Absolute Creator* seems to have created the entire system to know all happenings and even *It's Own Nature.* *It* must have done this with full consciousness and awareness. For, *It* also knows the method by which the system itself will unfold i.e. the route *It* (the deity) will have to take to understand even *It's* Own *Self.* In other words the Creator Itself knows and understands Its own Natural desire to know Itself, and completely understands Its own nature 'inside out'; It also knows the way *It* will have to take to fulfill *It's* own purpose and thus achieve *Self-fulfillment* i.e. *It* must re-create even *It's* own self to fully understand *It's* own nature. Now, *once It does that then It will get to fathom why it is in It's nature to 'create'. And since it is It's nature to create, It sets about creating a system to create Itself by replication. The entire process of EVOLUTION is but a means to replicate Itself. And as has been seen before, evolution is a continuous process of change. Change being the basis of, and necessity of Life. It is a perpetual cycle of self-improvement through evolution. Thus everything, even Nature Itself is in a process of constant evolution. It is the basis of the Al Hayio Al Qayyum (The Living, Eternal, Self-subsisting and Ever-Sustaining) nature of the Natural Deity.*

Were *It* not to know the means and method of re-becoming *Itself*, it would negate the hypothesis of belief that 'It is All-knowing and All-powerful'. *It*, in other words knows that the only way to Self-discovery is by Self-knowledge – which is gained by re-becoming *Itself*, or reverse engineering, and for which It has to start from the scratch or 'nothingness' and then go upwards and achieve 'everythingness'; or in other words to re-engineer Itself. This theory gets precedence from the idea developed in another essay ' Ultimate Human Reach'. Now, for a complete discovery of *Itself* the *Deity* has to begin from zero and traverse the entire path all along, and eventually attain infinity. For, as we have seen, that when two zeros merge they become infinity. God, who, if *It* is 'immanently indispensible', (Al Qur'an 112: 2) must of necessity, be the inherent and integral part of anything and everything. The need to be so is only explainable if *It* has a reason and purpose for being so. And the reason and purpose the Natural Creator has, is *It's* own Self-seeking and Self-desiring need to know 'Why' It does what It does. i.e. Why is it in *His* nature to create and Self-perpetuate and thus Self-fulfill? If this is not the case then there seems no reason for it to be Omniscient, Omnipresent and Omnipotent. Also, what would be the need for all the Creativity and the inherent desire of the created (humans) himself to seek their own purpose? Just reflect on this and observe man's own quest. For, he questions and seeks meaning in all things around him and his own being?

A 'Nature' that knows 'all' must have known that if It remained only in the paradigm of the meta-physics It would not Itself evolve into anything but remain an unconscious Being, and would eventually stay and perish into oblivion, having affected nothing not even Itself. So It says 'Kun,-- fa 'Yakun', Be! and it is (Al Qur'an 36: 82), This brings forth 'action and creativity', and Its own transformation, resulting in the beginning of the change of It's own paradigm, from the meta or unconscious, to the state of Physics or the beginning of consciousness; i.e. from Meta-physical to the Physical stage of It's own existence. This resulted in both the establishing of the Laws of Cause and Effect and as a consequence It's own change of state from the unconscious mode to the becoming of a Consciously Conscious Existence. The next stage in the cycle is the re-transference into the tranquil stage of becoming a Fully 'Conscious Being', fully appreciating and understanding It's own nature as to Why it does what It does i.e. 'Create'.

Seeing it another way the act of 'Creation' is the transforming of the potential energy content to the dynamic energy phase by the Deity of Its own Self. Hence 'dynamism' is the basis of the process of evolution whereas 'station' is stagnation. Thus, to consciously evolve one has to knowingly affect change in oneself -- do, or act or become dynamic from a state of stasis. This is the way to self fulfillment of both the created and the Creator Self of the two Selves.

If the Deity does not follow this line of reasoning would It not then, as mentioned earlier, be a mere egotistic puppeteer?

Before making our final conclusions it is worth looking at one interesting aspect of the phenomena of one of the many of Nature's creation – 'time'.

Again Ghalib says:

Nafas, maujj e muheet e baykhudee hai
Taghaful hai saaqi ka gila kaya

Time is a wave
In the depth of oblivion.
Why then complain of
The saqi's lack of attention.

Here Ghalib gives an original concept of time. He says time seems to be just a disturbance in the calm sea of everlasting tranquility; a temporary birth of consciousness in the void of serene, unconscious oblivion. This idea is far ahead of its own time, and its meaning and beauty is enhanced if seen in the light of the theory of relativity, which was propounded by Einstein about a hundred years later of Ghalib's quoted verse. Delving a little further on the thought, time seems to have started at the moment the Deity wished to seek Itself in a conscious manner i.e. at the instant It thought of becoming a consciously 'Conscious Being'. Waking up from 'Dormancy' to 'Enlightenment', turning from the 'potentiality' paradigm to 'dynamic mode'; or becoming conscious of the beauty of It's own creative ability, and then being desirous to fathom the reason why It has this attribute, and then the desire to show it to the world. In the second stanza says Ghailb says that, ' does it really matter if the saqi (the beautiful tavern hostess -- also signifying the dispenser of the elixir of life), forgot to pass a round of drinks' ? In other words we should not complain if the Creator turns *It's* attention momentarily from our needs, and seems to be disinterested in us. For, perhaps *It* has other more pressing preoccupations -- The search for *Itself.!*

Hence the conclusion is that the *Natural Deity is an integral part of all things and everything. It is an internal Controller, both affecting and being affected by the change within the system, because It is Itself the System -- maker of, yet subservient to Its own dictates.* It is this uniqueness or *singularity* of the Natural System, and the whole concept of **Al Haiyo Al Qayyum** – (Al Qur'an 2:255), i.e. *Living, Eternal, Self- subsisting and Ever-sustaining* nature of the Natural Deity, which keeps man guessing and wondering as to the nature of *Nature Itself*. However, it would only be fair to say that :- *'GOD'S alone is the perfect system, and systematic perfection leads to Godliness.*

Reflect upon Omar Khayyam's verse in light of the above essay, and A new fold meaning will ensue.

A moment guessed—then back behind the Fold
Immerst of Darkness round the Drama roll'd
Which, for the Pastime of Eternity,
He doth Himself contrive, enact, behold.

Chapter Sixteen

AN OPEN LETTER TO TERRORISTS

Dear fellow humans,
Some time ago I watched the launch of the Space shuttle 'Discovery'. The event was very captivating and exhilarating. There was a sense of uplift and accomplishment and a feeling of success at human achievement. The feeling of elation was beyond expression. All of mankind had reached a landmark of progress and self improvement. It strengthened my conviction in the human effort and its fruitful result for humanity as a whole. Around the same time I watched another event, and it was the London bombings. The effect of that had been just the reverse. It was sadness, remorse and dejection -- perhaps not so much at the reason for the act, as to its means and method. The event left a very bad taste in the mouth because, it showed the other side of human nature, that of man's intellectual degradation and self-abasement.

We humans are capable of so much in this world. We have achieved such lofty heights as traveling into outer space, and such lowly depths as self- destruction. We are capable of both *construction* and *destruction, rise* as much as *fall*. Which of these things we are destined for and aim to achieve? The destiny we choose for ourselves is eventually in our hands. Will we, as an evolved creation of Nature, further the frontiers of human achievement, or limit our own creative abilities and eventually destroy all that has been acquired? This will largely depend on our own thoughts and ideas, and finally the choice of our actions. True, the result of most action cannot be predicted before hand, yet the intention behind the act is in one's grasp. If the intention is constructive then the route to follow will have to be evolutionary; because most constructive acts are rather time consuming, difficult to come by, and are collective in nature. The launch into space did not come about in the wink of an eye. Devoted, painstaking effort on a collective level, chipped in by honest and humble human effort, brought about the event. The London bombings on the other hand were the outcome of meticulous secretive planning, stealth connivance, distorted belief and unleashing of cool calculated vengeance; Or perhaps, the blind effort of distorted belief. It may yet have been an act of twisted devotion and the premeditated taking of one's own life along with others, for a preconceived and an unknown reward.

The theory behind a revolutionary or destructive act is usually to eradicate the existing order, and to replace it by a new and radically different scenario. This mode of action somehow tends to forget that the establishment and strength of an ideology does not come from the way it is implemented, but from the inherent qualities of the idea itself. It is the idea that is the driving force and not the mode or means of establishing it. Also perhaps, the novelty of the idea alone is not the assurance of its success. Its timing and need of the environment is an important prerequisite for it to be established and durably entrenched. To achieve this, the selling of the idea is an important element in its promotion and propagation. Forcing a bitter pill down the throat is difficult and so most medicine is sugar coated to make it palatable. If there is hope in the efficacy of the drug it will be accepted even with some side effects, with an understanding that its beneficial action will eventually help cure the malady. All effort is made, and the treatment taken, with a hope and faith only in cure and betterment, not for destruction or death. For, once death comes all effort ends and no one knows for sure what the future may have in store. It is merely a conjecture and speculation to say that this or that happens after death. There is no proof or guarantee as no one has yet brought back any. Faith and belief are the primary means of humans to put the mental and intellectual misgivings to rest. If we have faith that goodness will eventually overcome evil, we should use the common good of humanity to fight the ills of society. Constructive action is one common goodness that can fight the evil of both within and without. Destruction is the common evil we have to avoid for it leads to the blind ally of the unknown.

Religious thought as discussed elsewhere, has itself developed and changed with human progress. The fundamentalists who practice religion in its most rigid form tend to stunt the growth of mental curiosity and intellectual probe, because they limit and restrain man at a lower level and God at a higher and altogether different station of abode. The one becomes the Creator and Controller and the other the subjugated and helplessly controlled. Also, religious orthodoxy inbreeds stagnation and unconscious ritualistic repetition. The natural outcome of unquestioned and blind ritual practice is introversive and becomes an end in itself, rather than being expressive, exploratory and a means to an end i.e. to lead towards self uplift and personal growth -- which must surely have been its primary aim for all Creation. Further, religious fundamentalism has negation as its basis. For it promotes religion by saying – 'don't do this', --'this is not allowed', -- 'That is against the rules'; etc. etc. Whereas the main aim of religious education should perhaps be to guide to the basis and the underlying need of various religious thought processes and disciplines. They should be able to advise how the practice of the ritual can lead towards its main aim of moral uplift and character building, which is essential for struggle and survival of a humane human race; and the eventual end game of *'good'* conquering *'evil'*. Constructive religious thought should be able to explain how the prayer is a road to the health and emancipation of the faculties of *mind, body* and *soul* -- the triad of human existence. That its essence lies not in performing of certain tenets, but in effect the releasing of the constructive juices of each one's personality and harmonizing the functions of the triad, so that one may gain fresher ideas and thoughts and grasp newer concepts, which would open and liberate the intellect rather than confine it. Religious education should be a means of accepting reality rather than fighting it. It should teach to welcome rather than reject realistic change. It should be educative and helpful in training humans to be able to harness their animal nature and direct it towards humanism and progress, and to eventually overcome the barbarism of within.

The core message of all religions is the same basic axioms of humanity. It is common observation that the basic instinct of a living being is to preserve life, its own first and then of the species. We humans, who are definitely more evolved than other creation, are so, because of our mind and intellect. These give us the edge and a capacity to consciously change both our selves and also our surroundings. If the change we bring about is in agreement with *'Nature's Plan'* and its basic laws of *'Cause* and *Effect'*, we will move towards progress. If however, we try to interfere and disturb the balance of the *'Natural scheme of things'* we will meet our own downfall and annihilation. This is so because it is in the *'nature of Nature'* to Self–preserve and Self-perpetuate.

A little closer study of humanity through history shows that humans continue to have the same basic animal instincts they have always possessed -- both good and bad e.g. the instinct of curiosity, competition, instinct of self-preservation, protection, destruction etc. Only those who have been able to understand and channelise these natural behaviours have stepped ahead and furthered the cause of the entire human race. It may be questioned whether humans have really progressed? They are still the most brutal and ruthless of creatures. They still have uncontrolled lust, and in reality have furthered their lustful pursuit, and so on and so forth. While all this is perhaps true, it may be pointed out that the basic instincts of human beings, because of their animal origin, will remain and continue to follow them. It is at the level of intellect that we can develop and advance, and its control over instincts improved. This comes about through the progressive and refining process of genetic inheritance coupled with the reforming aspect of knowledge and education. The advance or progress can thus be made at the level of *'thought'*. If the thought or intellect progresses it will lead to a conscious improvement of *'word'* and then eventually *'deed'*. For otherwise unconscious and untamed action is nothing but raw animal behaviour. Now, when intellectual development takes place, higher concepts can be grasped and understood and eventually put to use, contributing in the forward push of the frontiers of human achievement.

Human beings, like most creation, are constantly evolving. Man has come a long way from the cave and his way of doing things has radically changed. Further, the globe is not a patchwork of self - contained units as it was in the past. Technology and development has shrunk its size and brought down many natural and man-made barriers. It is now rapidly transforming into a global village. No part of it can live in isolation and not be influenced by the happenings in other areas. The methods and techniques of the old world have also changed and will continue to. Physical wars, which were rampant among nations in the earlier centuries have definitely decreased in number. It may be said that the world has taken up other kinds of wars, like economic, cultural or wars of ideas. The total elimination of wars is however an impossibility, because man, who basically possesses animal traits will not be completely free of them. Hate, anger and jealousies will continue to haunt us but their intensity and effect can be channelized and harnessed with knowledge and education, coupled with the reasoning power of the mind. It is also, none the less, a human trait to have an intellect -- the very tool which can make him self educate and improve. Like every thing else intellect shows two sides. It can lead to creativity or destruction, depending on the use it is put to. The basis of intellect is thoughts, and they can be both good and bad. Good thoughts originate in positive ideas and bad thoughts in negative ones. Positive ideas promote constructive change and negative ones lead to destruction and annihilation. Positivists are generally believers in themselves and the rest of mankind, whereas negativists are basically full of doubt and deception. They doubt themselves, all mankind, and are not sure of its purpose in the Natural phenomena.

Common sense prompts that the end of the ' World Scene' is perhaps not a cataclysmic destruction of the earth, as the plant itself may be a living entity as per the hypothesis of *Gaia*. The end may be the end of human life as we know it today. Yet the cosmos itself may evolve to something else. To what and how it will transform cannot be said with any certainty; here your guess is as good as mine. But since it has changed over the ages it shall presumably transform into something else in the future. From a positivist's point of view it should improve, get better and advance. From a negativist angle it should shrivel up and disintegrate. Our own activities on it will definitely play a part in the shaping of things to come. One of the positive effects of the intellect is to learn from experience, and utilize the knowledge gained for furthering the cause of the species and helping to bring about progress. Destruction and demolition are usually not positive traits, readjustment and refinement are. To eliminate and destroy an existing order would be to truncate and cut short any progress that may have been made so far. Real progress and durable change, as said earlier, require evolutionary means. It is accepted by everyone that peace is a better road to take than war. We humans may have to learnt it the hard way. The wars being presently fought are being increasingly exposed for their futility and insincerity of purpose. They will in the end, leave the aggressor more exhausted, fruitlessly consumed by bloated avarice, perhaps a loser in the long run. The future cannot be predicted, but the past can be reflected upon and lessons learnt from history. What we need to do in this shrinking world is to pool our strengths of information and knowledge to promote broad based exchange of ideas for a common goal. We must learn from the lessons of history, to develop democracy and avoid unilateral dictatorial decisions, and to learn to consult and cooperate and avoid coercion and force.

The world bodies like the League of Nations have given way to more evolved International organizations as the United Nations. True, that the existing setup itself does not seem an ideal Organization, but it too is evolving and is bound to change to accept the realities of the shrinking world. The classical media of the screen and the press have been virtually overhauled due to globalization. The World Wide Web and the Internet have developed into sources of multidimensional communication. This has made each of us both more independent yet more dependent on one another, as everyone is able to directly participate in many events as they occur on the globe. Such a possibility was not even dreamed of until quite recently. The full potential of this tool has perhaps yet to be fathomed and much more interaction and exchange at the individual level is yet to come about. With more independence comes more freedom. Yet to every action there is an equal and balancing reaction, and more freedom will entail more responsibility and self-restraint. In the long run each of us will be held far more responsible for our actions than was ever possible in the past. The only way to sustain further growth would be to voluntarily share and give rather than grab or coerce. To share, each of us will have to make conscious and willing sacrifice from whatever we possess or are capable of acquiring. So far the world has managed to survive on the theory of 'Survival of the fittest'. It must soon realize that the 'fittest' would be one, who not only makes the most, but who is willing to part with most of the surplus, for the benefit of the species as a whole. Ones fitness will now have to be gauged on the scale of sharing and giving rather than acquiring and accumulating. This change of attitude will first require a change of heart and mind at the level of each individual. We have to learn to understand the difference and the correlation between Passion and Capability, Emotion and Sensibility, and Independence and Interdependence. In a nut-shell human beings have to learn to maintain a voluntary balance between desire and need, which has been fully exploited by the evils of marketing by promoting our desires and making us succumb to them as if they were really our needs. In short, we have to learn not only to live but also to keep each other alive at the same time.

It is in the above scenario that each of us has to adjust, and knowingly and willingly change our ways, for we will be ready to change them only if we know and realize that we must change them. We have to persevere to preserve and not pervert what we have. What goes around comes around. Destruction breeds and perpetuates itself. Democracy is the only way to the future, and it will have to flourish if the world is to survive as a single unit for human existence. The old mode and means of governance and power-play are bound to cave in if the human race is to survive in the change and transformation that is taking place at the global scene. True, that democracy itself is in a state of evolution and must readjust in the favour of the 'have-nots' , as the 'haves' till now, have had more than their share. We, each of us can now play our part and give our opinion in the matter of readjustment as this concerns every single one of us. But again, we must remember that we should agree to disagree in ideas alone, for we will have to agree to a joint act to preserve the species as a whole. This, as said earlier, is imperative because from a positivist's approach the human species is perhaps not created for unfounded annihilation. For, if it were so, the whole exercise of creationism would become meaningless. It only makes logical sense if it were founded on the idea of progress and evolution into the next higher stage of existence. Self-inflicted destruction is not the answer; Self-preservation is the key in the fulfillment of this prophecy.

With good wishes from a fellow human.

Ziauddin Ahmed
tidylink@yahoo.com

Chapter Seventeen
LIFE AFTER DEATH

Human existence does not come to an end after death of physical life. There is surely some form of existence even after that state. It would be meaningless if life were to come to an end abruptly. All the work of Nature in bringing about this life and its evolution would then seem to have been of no purpose. The entire exercise of Creativity of Nature would become meaningless. The only thing that ends at death is the ability to act and perform physical activity. This is so because physical life is the final evolutionary stage of material life and it is this matter that stays behind and finally turns into dust from whence it came forth. The other two faculties of humans i.e. mind and soul seem to be preserved and taken forward into the next phase of existence.

Scientifically all activity began with the event of the Big Bang-- some fourteen billion years ago. A process of Change started and then all things began to evolve. Matter itself underwent a slow progress, and different kind of things began to appear. The table of elements saw the development of matter itself. Most living matter is primarily the outcome of various processes of the permutation and combination, primarily of the elements of Oxygen, Hydrogen and Carbon. Living things started with the presence of matter in water at suitable temperatures, and due to the interaction of some form of energy with it.

The triad of body, mind and soul should be in harmonic function for the human to remain alive. The triad is like the functioning of the computer where the three things essential for it to be operative are the hardware, the software and an electrical impulse. When the impulse is stopped or cut off there is no life in the computer. This is similar to human life. When the soul escapes the body it becomes lifeless. Thus the soul is the very impulse of Nature, It's Energy which penetrates and permeates the body and keeps it alive. The physical structure of a person may still remain behind at death; but it is like the computer box which is unable to function without the electric impulse. Both the mind and the body are incapable of functioning without the soul. When the current is switched off the computer cannot act on the software which is, however, always present in cyber space, just like the mind. It can begin to make its effect felt as soon as the hard ware is provided the energy or the electrical impulse.

If the mind is seen as a source rather than the by-product of the brain it can remain functional even after death. That is to say that the mind is the basis of life and that thoughts are the primary source of its communication with life, Whereas the brain is the receptor of these thoughts and provides meaning to them through physical action.

The brain can be analogous to the hardware of a computer and the mind to the software which runs the computer-- the brain. The soul then becomes the impulse of energy needed to run the whole system. The origination of thoughts' is in the Cosmic Mind and is the essence of Nature Itself. They are like electro-magnetic impulses floating in the atmosphere around us. They are captured by the brain which can be tuned to receive them. This is a similar process to the reception of signals by hardware like computers, radio, television etc.

Each one of us is unique and is an individual, and thus has a unique capacity to think and capture independent and particular thoughts. These thoughts are floating in the meta-physical realm and are always available in cyber space. Now, only when a thought impinges on the brain it sets the brain to start to function and produces chemical reactions in it. These reactions produce impulses in the brain cells, which travel through them and carry various messages to different parts of the body. The body then begins to act or respond accordingly. Upon physical death the brain stops to function and dies, and is incapable of receiving the messages any further or to process the thoughts impinging upon it. It so happens because the all important 'impulse' has stopped to flow. Once this happens the physical portion or the body remains behind and becomes dormant and loses its capability to act. Death, thus only ends physical action and the mind and the soul escape from it and so man becomes lifeless, incapable of performing any physical action. Now, if the mind was the function of the brain then all mental activity should culminate with death and there would be no residual effect left behind of the life that was lived. There would also be no effect on the life of other human beings. This does not seem to be the case as the dead person does leave behind some effect on the earth and even on the lives of others. The effect left behind on this earth is of a physical nature, whereas the effect on other human beings can be both physical and non-physical, or spiritual.

We humans are thinking beings, and our thoughts are capable of affecting and interacting with one another. This interaction forms a chain of cause and effect, i.e. one person's thoughts can become the cause of the other person to act or react, or so to say that thoughts of one affect the others, both the living and the dead. The living may undergo both physical and meta-physical change whereas the dead are affected at the meta-physical level alone.

When a person dies, others that have interacted with him continue to carry thoughts of and about the dead person. These thoughts wane off with the passage of time because of the brain's nature of forgetfulness. Were it not be so, life would be impossible to bear and would become a living hell. One prays for the departed soul, thinking that the prayer will have affect on it and give it some sort of solace. This maybe so, but in fact the prayer primarily gives relief to the one who is praying, for we do not know for certain what effect it produces on the dead person. The intensity of thought and feelings depend on the intensity of relationship between the living and the dead. The closer one has been in association with the dead person the more intense would have been the feelings between the two. This intensity of feelings or emotions lives on in the form of a strong memory that lingers after the parting between the two. The dead and the living are in two different realms or phases of existence, and their communication must also be in a meta-physical or a supernatural way. They communicate through the language of the souls, because the souls are interlinked and are joined in the other phase of existence. This assumption is based on the logic of continuity and connection of existence of all things. The language of communication is at the level of the mind as the bodies have separated and their material aspect is left behind on earth.

Minds can communicate with other minds in a number of ways. In the living it is through thoughts, which can be communicated both through languages and other ways and methods. The other ways of communication of thoughts may be through feelings and emotions in a metaphysical or spiritual form. Though thoughts are meta-physical in nature they can take on a material shape when communicated through the language of words, which can then be transmitted though technological means from one place to another. Thoughts may also be transferred non-physically. There may be non-verbal transfer of ideas from one person to the other. These methods can be felt and imagined better in non-physical terms, rather than physically. Things like love, emotions and feelings are means of such transfer of thoughts. Thoughts and ideas do not die, they do go into some form of oblivion if not put into practice; but when they are acted upon they leave physical effects, for otherwise they stay in the meta-physical state.

The mind is continually functioning at all times because it is always present out there in cyber space. Thoughts are the minds method of communication from 'Nature' to the receptor – the brain. When one is awake the brain is capturing thoughts at the conscious level. However, the brain is not receptive to conscious thoughts of the Mind during the stage of sleep or rest. This is the period when the brain is dormant or is switched off and is perhaps reconstructing itself for the next day's job. Thoughts are never the less always floating in cyber space. Dreams are the functioning of the mind when it is working at a sub-conscious level. Dreams come in a state when the brain is coming out of dormancy or sleep to just near awakening. The dreams may reflect the experiences of the waking life or may be wild imaginations and feelings one may never have knowingly thought about.

The mind is capable of permuting and combining all information the brain gathers in its memory. This it can do by using its power to fathom and manipulate the messages from cyber space. This is like the RAM (random access memory) of a computer. This permutation and combination of ideas in the brain give the person his/her innovative quality. The brain can be made to capture, remember, discover, invent and innovate, but it cannot create them. Creation is the Domain of the Creator alone. In other words the brain has the capability of RO (read only) function of a computer. Once having created, Nature sends forth vibrations and pulses into cyber space which are then captured by the individual's brain as according to its strength and capacity. The brain, none the less, has the capability to grow further. It develops with the change of circumstance and the experience gained by the humans with the passage of time. The mind and the brain go hand in hand to enhance the capacity and capability of a person. Like other things in nature the brain can evolve and improve itself within the frame work of the 'laws of Nature'. The soul is another aspect of human existence which goes on living after death. The soul is an infinitesimal extension of the Universal Spirit Itself, that which pervades the Universe in all its manifestations. The soul is the very essence of Creation and it cannot be created or destroyed. It is eternal in its existence. It's metamorphoses is most beautifully explained in the Quran.

For it says thus:

The soul
and how it is integrated (with the body)
And given the faculty
of knowing what is disruptive
and what is intrinsic to it.
He who nourishes it
Will surely be successful,
And he who confines it
Will certainly come to grief.
(Al Quran 91,7-10)

The soul is so well integrated with matter that it seeps and penetrates in every nook and corner of a body, be it living or inanimate. The soul is the very essence of each and everything and cannot be separated except at death or transfer into the next paradigm. The soul is eternal and when a body dies its soul is transferred to another form of existence in another paradigm, going back to its original Source.

All things are interconnected through their souls. The soul also seems to influence and is in turn influenced by other souls. The influence on one another depends on the relationship that has existed between one soul and the other. This relationship may be due to the effect of different people coming in contact during their lifetime on this earth. It may also be a metaphysical relationship with powerful souls gone before in time to the other paradigm. The soul also has the quality of entanglement, whereby one soul may be entangled (a term better explained by quantum Physics)to another one in this world or out of it. The final abode of all souls is in Nature Itself. And as Nature is continuous, therefore, it is assumed that so must be at all souls. They have been residing in oblivion or some kind of a background, till they get an identity of an entity at the time of birth into physical life.

Reflect on what Ghalib says in:-

Nafas, maujj e muheet e baykhudee hai
Taghaful hai saaqi ka gila kaya

Time (individual soul or consciousness) is a wave
In the depth of oblivion.
Why then complain of
The saqi's lack of attention.

(Here Ghalib gives an original concept of soul, time or consciousness. He says soul, time or consciousness seems to be just a disturbance in the calm sea of everlasting tranquility; a temporary birth of consciousness in the void of unconscious oblivion. This idea is far ahead of its own time, and its meaning and beauty is enhanced if seen in the light of the theory of relativity, which was propounded by Einstein about a hundred years later. Delving a little further on the thought, time seems to have started at the moment the Deity wished to seek Itself in a conscious manner i.e. at the instant It thought of becoming a consciously 'Conscious Being'. Waking up from 'Dormancy' to 'Enlightenment', or becoming conscious of the beauty of It's own creative ability, and then being desirous to show it to the world. {This concept has been discussed in greater detail in my essay, '*Nature of a Natural Deity*'. In the second stanza says Ghailb says that, 'does it really matter if the saqi (the beautiful tavern hostess) forgot to pass a round of drinks' ? In other words we should not complain if the Creator turns His attention momentarily from our needs, and seems to be disinterested in us.

In the above stanza, if '*time*' were to be replaced by '*soul*' or '*consciousness*' then a new fold meaning would ensue, and that is that, 'being born', means to come out of the oblivion of unconsciousness to awareness of the surroundings. That a person experiencing this life and his individual circumstance gives his *soul* a kind of *awareness,* a *consciousness* of some sort, and this awareness does not get lost, but goes in the next phase of existence. It remains even after earthly life may have come to an end.

We interact with each other and everything else in some form. The effect of this interaction is also felt at the meta-physical level and leaves meta-physical effects, which can be transferred to physical activity by the minds function through the brain, as explained earlier. It seems we radiate and send out vibrations in all directions and influence who and whatever comes in our field of influence. In turn we are affected by the others' fields.

This field of influence is somewhat like a field of influence of a magnet or an electric field. The stronger is the source the stronger is its field and hence the more powerful is the effect. The strength of a person's field or force depends on the strength of his/her personality. This personality develops with the passage of time, and in human beings it can be strengthened with the performance of conscious action. If good and constructive acts are performed the development takes place in a positive direction, but if bad and destructive actions are promoted the personality grows with a strong negative field and consequently it's effect and influence will have evil repercussions. When we interact with each other we leave some conscious or unconscious effect on one another. If the interaction is strong and severe it affects even the souls and an indelible impression is left behind. The strength of interaction depends on the influence of the one on the other; meaning, that if a strong personality is interacting with another strong personality the influence on both will be of strength. This interaction can become a strong bond if both are of a similar polarity; but if the reaction is between two opposing polarities it will be a clash of fields of opposite nature and will result in opposition of thoughts and ideas, and eventually deeds or action. Progress and evolution is the result when two similar polarities interact with each other, but destruction and devolution is the result of a clash of opposite personalities.

It has been ingrained in human nature to pursue the progression of its triad of mind, body and soul. The three have to remain in balance and harmony to maintain a healthy human being. If the balance is disturbed the body reacts and gets distorted. Some of us may, however, be more developed in one element of the triad at a given time. We are not all identical, some may develop more in the physique, whereas some others may be more enhanced in the spiritual side. However, there is propensity of change in each of us and we can direct this change both consciously as well as sub-consciously.

The real purpose of creation is somehow the fulfillment of Nature Itself; just as every human's nature, which is also to seek it's own fulfillment. We feel fulfilled when we become conscious and rediscover ourselves. Nature also gets this Self fulfillment when It rediscovers Itself. To rediscover Itself Nature sought to recreate and replicate Itself by reverse engineering. This It will do by waking from slumber of unconsciousness to become an enlightened Entity. (This is central theme of the essay of my other essay, 'Nature of a natural Deity'.)

It is God who, Himself, lives through man and views every trial and tribulation man undertakes in this life. After having acquired the experience through living, humans carry the awareness and its effects to the next phase of existence and passes them on to the 'data bank' of Nature Itself. In other words we live in a participatory Universe where the Creator and the created are entangled; each participating to the benefit of the other. The universe is one. According to Physics any part of the universe is an observer and each part is interacting with the other. Observation, in Physics, is actually interaction and all things are observers, all are interacting with each other. Observation and interaction is really information exchange through an imaginary boundary. (Idea extrapolated from the lecture on entanglement by Chris Fields, on YouTube). Just like the bits of information are indestructible as per science, so the information stored in the memory is indestructible. This information is transferred at death from one paradigm to the next phase of existence. The total compilation is all the time being accumulated in the data-bank of the Kosmos (or Nature) Itself.

So at death there is just a transfer from the physical state of existence to a meta-physical form of existence. There must have been an existence before birth, which was an unconscious stage of life. In this state one was living at a meta-physical level as a part of the Cosmic Soul, and had not yet acquired an identity or a separate individual shape. At conception, a physical manifestation takes place with the incorporation of a soul in the fetus, in the womb of a mother. This is the unconsciously conscious phase of existence. From birth to death one lives a life in this world at a consciously conscious level of existence and acquires awareness and knowledge. At death one is transferred from a conscious to an unconscious form of existence, taking with it the awareness and memory of the life it lived on earth. Thus life after death is nothing but another phase of existence. Only this time it is aware and conscious of the life it lived on earth.

Author's Profile

ZIAUDDIN AHMED hails from Karachi, Pakistan, where he grew up and got his education. He completed B.Sc.(Hons) and M.Sc. from Karachi University. He started his career as a teacher in Karachi Grammar School. He then worked with a number of multinationals including Unilever at home and abroad. He migrated to Canada in 1989. He is the author of 'Thought Provoking Essays' published by iUniverse, USA., which has been revised and expanded recently and is titled ' Towards Rational Belief '. He had earlier compiled 'Celestial Marriage', a new age commentary on Islam.

He has translated selections of Mirza Ghalib, the famous poet of India, into English, under the title of GHALIB – (AS I UNDERSTAND HIM). He has made a number of reviews and commentaries of other authors' work. He is associated with many literary, cultural and Social groups in Canada.

Printed in the USA
CPSIA information can be obtained
at www.ICGtesting.com
LVHW071818230824
789091LV00017B/267